UPDATED AND REVISED EDITION

Celebrate Recovery®

PARTICIPANT'S GUIDE
VOLUMES 1–4

THE JOURNEY BEGINS

John Baker, along with his wife Cheryl, founded Celebrate Recovery®, a ministry started at Saddleback Church in 1991. John was on staff from the time Celebrate Recovery started until he went home to be with Jesus in 2021. He served as the Pastor of Membership, the Pastor of Ministries, and the Pastor of Saddleback Church's Signature Ministries. He also served as one of the nine Elder Pastors at Saddleback. John was a nationally known speaker and trainer in helping churches start Celebrate Recovery ministries. John's writing accomplishments include Celebrate Recovery's *The Journey Begins* Curriculum, *Life's Healing Choices*, the *Celebrate Recovery Study Bible* (general editor), and *The Landing* and *Celebration Place* (coauthor), *Your First Step to Celebrate Recovery* and *The Celebrate Recovery Daily Devotional* (coauthor). John and Cheryl were married for more than five decades and served together in Celebrate Recovery since the beginning. They have two adult children, Laura and Johnny, and five grandchildren.

Johnny Baker is the Global Executive Director of Celebrate Recovery, along with his wife Jeni. He has been on staff at Celebrate Recovery since 2004 and has been the Pastor of Celebrate Recovery at Saddleback Church since 2012. As an adult child of an alcoholic who chose to become an alcoholic himself, Johnny is passionate about breaking the cycle of dysfunction in his family and helping other families find the tools that will lead to healing and openness. He knows that because of Jesus Christ, and by continuing to stay active in Celebrate Recovery, Maggie, Chloe, and Jimmy—his three children—will never see him drink. Johnny is a nationally recognized speaker, trainer, and teacher of Celebrate Recovery. He is the author of *Road to Freedom*, a coauthor of the *Celebrate Recovery Daily Devotional*, *Celebration Place*, and *The Landing*, and is an associate editor of the *Celebrate Recovery Study Bible*. Johnny and Jeni have been married since 2000.

UPDATED AND REVISED EDITION

Celebrate Recovery®

PARTICIPANT'S GUIDE
VOLUMES 1–4

THE JOURNEY BEGINS

A recovery program based on eight principles from the Beatitudes

JOHN BAKER

FOREWORD BY RICK WARREN

Celebrate Recovery Participant's Guides, Volumes 1–4

©1998, 2012, 2025 by John Baker

Published in Grand Rapids, Michigan, by HarperChristian Resources. HarperChristian Resources is a registered trademark of HarperCollins Christian Publishing, Inc.

Requests for information should be sent to customercare@harpercollins.com.

ISBN 978-0-310-17597-1 (softcover)
ISBN 978-0-310-17598-8 (ebook)

All Scripture quotations are taken from the Holy Bible, New International Version®, NIV®. Copyright © 1973, 1978, 1984, 2011 by Biblica, Inc.® Used by permission. All rights reserved worldwide.

Any internet addresses (websites, blogs, etc.) and telephone numbers in this study guide are offered as a resource. They are not intended in any way to be or imply an endorsement by HarperChristian Resources, nor does HarperChristian Resources vouch for the content of these sites and numbers for the life of this study guide.

All rights reserved. No portion of this book may be reproduced, stored in a retrieval system, or transmitted in any form or by any means—electronic, mechanical, photocopy, recording, scanning, or other—except for brief quotations in critical reviews or articles, without the prior written permission of the publisher.

HarperChristian Resources titles may be purchased in bulk for church, business, fundraising, or ministry use. For information, please e-mail ResourceSpecialist@ChurchSource.com.

First Printing March 2025 / Printed in the United States of America

Foreword by Rick Warren	vii
The Road to Recovery	ix
Twelve Steps and Their Biblical Comparisons	x
Serenity Prayer	xiii
Celebrate Recovery's Small Group Guidelines	xv
Volume 1, Introduction	2
Volume 1, Lesson 1: Denial	3
Volume 1, Lesson 2: Powerless	9
Volume 1, Lesson 3: Hope	17
Volume 1, Lesson 4: Sanity	21
Volume 1, Lesson 5: Turn	27
Volume 1, Lesson 6: Action	31
Volume 1, Congratulations and Next Step	37
Volume 2, Introduction	40
Volume 2, Lesson 7: Sponsor	41
Volume 2, Lesson 8: Moral	47
Volume 2, Lesson 9: Inventory	53
Volume 2, Lesson 10: Spiritual Inventory Part 1	61
Volume 2, Lesson 11: Spiritual Inventory Part 2	69
Volume 2, Congratulations and Next Step	76
Volume 3, Introduction	78
Volume 3, Lesson 12: Confess	79
Volume 3, Lesson 13: Admit	85
Volume 3, Lesson 14: Ready	91
Volume 3, Lesson 15: Victory	97

Volume 3, Lesson 16: Amends 103
Volume 3, Lesson 17: Forgiveness 109
Volume 3, Lesson 18: Grace 115
Volume 3, Congratulations and Next Step 122

Volume 4, Introduction 124
Volume 4, Lesson 19: Crossroads 125
Volume 4, Lesson 20: Daily Inventory 137
Volume 4, Lesson 21: Relapse 145
Volume 4, Lesson 22: Gratitude 153
Volume 4, Lesson 23: Give 161
Volume 4, Lesson 24: Yes 167
Volume 4, Lesson 25: Seven Reasons We Get Stuck 173

Congratulations and Closing Word 176

Foreword by Rick Warren

You've undoubtedly heard the expression "Time heals all wounds." Unfortunately, it isn't true. As a pastor I frequently talk with people who are still carrying hurts from thirty or forty years ago. The truth is, time often makes things worse. Wounds that are left untended fester and spread infection throughout your entire body. Time only extends the pain if the problem isn't dealt with.

Celebrate Recovery® is a biblical and balanced program that can help you overcome your hurts, habits, and hang-ups. Based on the actual words of Jesus rather than psychological theory, this recovery program is more effective in helping people change than anything else I've seen or heard of. Over the years I've witnessed how the Holy Spirit has used this program to transform literally thousands of lives at Saddleback Church and help people grow toward full Christlike maturity.

Perhaps you are familiar with the classic 12-Step program of AA and other groups. While undoubtedly many lives have been helped through the 12 Steps, I've always been uncomfortable with that program's vagueness about the nature of God, the saving power of Jesus Christ, and the ministry of the Holy Spirit. So I began an intense study of the Scriptures to discover what God had to say about "recovery." To my amazement, I found the principles of recovery—in their logical order—given by Christ in His most famous message, the Sermon on the Mount.

My study resulted in a ten-week series of messages called "The Road to Recovery." During that series my associate pastor John Baker developed the four participant's guides, which became the heart of our Celebrate Recovery program.

As you work through these four volumes in this participant's guide, I trust that you will come to realize many benefits from this program. Most of all, however, my prayer for you is that, through Celebrate Recovery, you will find deep peace and lasting freedom in Jesus Christ as you walk your own road to recovery.

Dr. Rick Warren
Founder of Saddleback Church

The Road to Recovery

EIGHT PRINCIPLES BASED ON THE BEATITUDES

By Pastor Rick Warren

1. **R**ealize I'm not God. I admit that I am powerless to control my tendency to do the wrong thing and that my life is unmanageable.
    Blessed are the poor in spirit, for theirs is the kingdom of heaven. (Matthew 5:3)
2. **E**arnestly believe that God exists, that I matter to Him, and that He has the power to help me recover.
    Blessed are those who mourn, for they will be comforted. (Matthew 5:4)
3. **C**onsciously choose to commit all my life and will to Christ's care and control.
    Blessed are the meek, for they will inherit the earth. (Matthew 5:5)
4. **O**penly examine and confess my hurts, hang-ups, and habits to myself, to God, and to someone I trust.
    Blessed are the pure in heart, for they will see God. (Matthew 5:8)
5. **V**oluntarily submit to every change God wants to make in my life and humbly ask Him to remove my character defects.
    Blessed are those who hunger and thirst for righteousness, for they will be filled. (Matthew 5:6)
6. **E**valuate all my relationships. Offer forgiveness to those who have hurt me and make amends for harm I've done to others, except when to do so would harm them or others.
    Blessed are the merciful, for they will be shown mercy. (Matthew 5:7)
    Blessed are the peacemakers, for they will be called children of God. (Matthew 5:9)
7. **R**eserve a daily time with God for self-examination, Bible reading, and prayer in order to know God and His will for my life and to gain the power to follow His will.
8. **Y**ield myself to God to be used to bring this Good News to others, both by my example and by my words.
    Blessed are those who are persecuted because of righteousness, for theirs is the kingdom of heaven. (Matthew 5:10)

Twelve Steps and Their Biblical Comparisons[1]

1. We admitted we were powerless over our addictions and compulsive behaviors, that our lives had become unmanageable.

    For I know that good itself does not dwell in me, that is, in my sinful nature. For I have the desire to do what is good, but I cannot carry it out. (Romans 7:18)

2. We came to believe that a power greater than ourselves could restore us to sanity.

    For it is God who works in you to will and to act in order to fulfill his good purpose. (Philippians 2:13)

3. We made a decision to turn our lives and our wills over to the care of God.

    Therefore, I urge you, brothers and sisters, in view of God's mercy, to offer your bodies as a living sacrifice, holy and pleasing to God—this is your true and proper worship. (Romans 12:1)

4. We made a searching and fearless moral inventory of ourselves.

    Let us examine our ways and test them, and let us return to the Lord. (Lamentations 3:40)

5. We admitted to God, to ourselves, and to another human being the exact nature of our wrongs.

    Therefore confess your sins to each other and pray for each other so that you may be healed. (James 5:16)

---

[1]. Throughout this material, you will notice several references to the Christ-centered 12 Steps. Our prayer is that Celebrate Recovery will create a bridge to the millions of people who are familiar with the secular 12 Steps (I acknowledge the use of some material from the 12 Suggested Steps of Alcoholics Anonymous.) and in so doing, introduce them to the one and only true Higher Power, Jesus Christ. Once they begin that relationship, asking Christ into their hearts as Lord and Savior, true healing and recovery can begin!

6. We were entirely ready to have God remove all these defects of character.

    Humble yourselves before the Lord, and he will lift you up. (James 4:10)

7. We humbly asked Him to remove all our shortcomings.

    If we confess our sins, he is faithful and just and will forgive us our sins and purify us from all unrighteousness. (1 John 1:9)

8. We made a list of all persons we had harmed and became willing to make amends to them all.

    Do to others as you would have them do to you. (Luke 6:31)

9. We made direct amends to such people whenever possible, except when to do so would injure them or others.

    "Therefore, if you are offering your gift at the altar and there remember that your brother or sister has something against you, leave your gift there in front of the altar. First go and be reconciled to them; then come and offer your gift." (Matthew 5:23–24)

10. We continued to take personal inventory and when we were wrong, promptly admitted it.

    So, if you think you are standing firm, be careful that you don't fall! (1 Corinthians 10:12)

11. We sought through prayer and meditation to improve our conscious contact with God, praying only for knowledge of His will for us and power to carry that out.

    Let the message of Christ dwell among you richly. (Colossians 3:16)

12. Having had a spiritual experience as the result of these steps, we try to carry this message to others and to practice these principles in all our affairs.

    Brothers and sisters, if someone is caught in a sin, you who live by the Spirit should restore that person gently. But watch yourselves, or you also may be tempted. (Galatians 6:1)

Serenity Prayer

If you have attended secular recovery programs, you have seen the first four lines of the "Prayer for Serenity." The following is the complete prayer. I encourage you to pray it daily as you work through the principles!

Prayer for Serenity

God, grant me the serenity
to accept the things I cannot change,
the courage to change the things I can,
and the wisdom to know the difference.
Living one day at a time,
enjoying one moment at a time;
accepting hardship as a pathway to peace; taking, as Jesus did,
this sinful world as it is,
not as I would have it;
trusting that You will make all things right
if I surrender to Your will;
so that I may be reasonably happy in this life and supremely happy with You forever in
    the next. Amen.

Reinhold Niebuhr

Celebrate Recovery's Small Group Guidelines

The following five guidelines will ensure that your small group is a safe place. They need to be read at the beginning of every meeting.

1. Keep your sharing focused on your own thoughts and feelings using "I" and "me" statements. Limit your sharing to three to five minutes.
2. There is NO cross talk. Cross talk is when two individuals engage in conversation excluding all others. Each person is free to express his or her feelings without interruptions.
3. We are here to support one another, not "fix" one another.
4. Anonymity and confidentiality are basic requirements. What is shared in the group stays in the group. The only exception is when someone threatens to injure themselves or others.
5. Offensive language has no place in a Christ-centered recovery group.

The following guidelines are to be used in all online Open Share Groups and Step studies.

6. **All members must use headphones.** This will ensure that no one else can overhear what is shared in the group.
7. **All members must be on camera and alone in the room,** with the camera facing them the whole time. If the group leader asks, they must show the rest of the group that no one else is in the room.
8. **The meetings will not be recorded.** This protects the condentiality and anonymity of the meetings.

   Emphasize at the close of your meeting that Guidelines stay intact as participants fellowship with each other after the meeting.

Stepping Out of Denial and Into God's Grace

Introduction

Welcome to the "Road to Recovery." You are in for an exciting and amazing journey as you take the hand of the true and only Higher Power, Jesus Christ, and walk with Him toward healing and serenity.

The purpose of this program is to allow us to become free from life's hurts, hang-ups, and habits. By working through the eight recovery principles found in the Beatitudes with Jesus Christ as your Higher Power, you can and will change! You will begin to experience the true peace and serenity you have been seeking, and you will no longer have to rely on your dysfunctional, compulsive, and addictive behaviors as a temporary "fix" for your pain.

By applying the biblical principles of conviction, conversion, surrender, confession, restitution, prayer, quiet time, witnessing, and helping one another, which are found within the eight principles and the Christ-centered 12 Steps, you will restore and develop stronger relationships with others and with God.

To begin our journey, we will need to step out of denial and into God's grace. This is what working through Principles 1–3 will help us accomplish. We begin by looking at the toll *denial* has had on our ability to face the reality of our past and present. Then we need to admit that we are *powerless* over certain areas of our lives, and that, alone, we do not have the power to control them.

In Principle 2, we find the *hope* that our Higher Power, Jesus Christ, can restore us to sanity and that through Him alone we can find the power to help us recover. And finally, in Principle 3, we take the *action* to *turn* our lives and our wills over to His care and direction.

After each lesson, there is an exercise for you to complete. Answer each question to the best of your ability. Don't worry about what you think the answer *should* be. Pray and then write down the answer from your heart. Remember John 8:32: "Then you will know the truth, and the truth will set you free."

After you have completed the exercise, share it with someone you trust. Your group, an accountability partner, your sponsor (someone farther along in recovery who has agreed to be your "travel guide"; sponsors are explained in Volume 2, Lesson 7), or a close friend in recovery are all choices. You do not recover from your hurts, hang-ups, and habits just by attending recovery meetings. You must work and live following the eight principles of recovery found in the Beatitudes and the 12 Steps and their biblical comparisons. God bless you as you walk this road.

In His steps,
John Baker

LESSON 1

Denial

Principle 1: Realize I'm not God. I admit that I am powerless to control my tendency to do the wrong thing and that my life is unmanageable.

Blessed are the poor in spirit, for theirs is the kingdom of heaven. (Matthew 5:3)

Step 1: We admitted we were powerless over our addictions and compulsive behaviors, that our lives had become unmanageable.

For I know that good itself does not dwell in me, that is, in my sinful nature. For I have the desire to do what is good, but I cannot carry it out. (Romans 7:18)

Think About It

Before we can take the first step of our recovery, we must first face and admit our denial. You can't heal a wound by saying it's not there. The acrostic for DENIAL spells out what can happen if we do not face our denial.

Disables our feelings

By repressing our feelings we freeze our emotions. Understanding and feeling our feelings is freedom.

They promise them freedom, while they themselves are slaves of depravity—for "people are slaves to whatever has mastered them." (2 Peter 2:19)

Energy lost

A side effect of our denial is anxiety. Anxiety causes us to waste precious energy running from our past and worrying about and dreading the future. It is only in the present, today, where positive change can occur.

He upholds the cause of the oppressed and gives food to the hungry. The LORD sets prisoners free, the LORD gives sight to the blind, the LORD lifts up those who are bowed down, the LORD loves the righteous. (Psalm 146:7–8)

Negates growth

We are "as sick as our secrets." We cannot grow in recovery until we are ready to step out of our denial into the truth.

Then they cried to the LORD in their trouble, and he saved them from their distress. He brought them out of darkness, the utter darkness, and broke away their chains. Let them give thanks to the LORD for his unfailing love and his wonderful deeds for mankind, for he breaks down gates of bronze and cuts through bars of iron. (Psalms 107:13–16)

Isolates us from God

God's light shines on the truth. Our denial keeps us in the dark.

DENIAL

This is the message we have heard from him and declare to you: God is light; in him there is no darkness at all. If we claim to have fellowship with him and yet walk in the darkness, we lie and do not live out the truth. But if we walk in the light, as he is in the light, we have fellowship with one another, and the blood of Jesus, his Son, purifies us from all sin. (1 John 1:5–7)

Alienates us from our relationships

Denial tells us we are getting away with it. We think no one knows—but they do. What is the answer?

Therefore each of you must put off falsehood and speak truthfully to your neighbor, for we are all members of one body. (Ephesians 4:25)

Lengthens the pain

We have the false belief that denial protects us from our pain. In reality, denial allows our pain to fester and grow and turn into *shame* and *guilt*.

*When I kept silent, my bones wasted away through my groaning all day long. For day and night your hand was heavy on me; my strength was sapped as in the heat of summer. Then I acknowledged my sin to you and did not cover up my iniquity. I said, "I will confess my transgressions to the L*ord*." And you forgave the guilt of my sin. (Psalm 32:3–5)*

Accept the first principle of recovery. Step out of your denial! Step into your Higher Power's—Jesus Christ's—unconditional love and grace!

Write About It

1. What areas of your life do you have power (control) over? Be specific.

2. What areas of your life are out of control, unmanageable? Be specific.

3. How do you think taking this first step will help you?

4. As a child, what coping skills did you use to protect yourself or get attention?

5. In your family of origin, what was the "family secret" that everyone was trying to protect?

6. How do you handle pain and disappointment?

DENIAL

7. How can you begin to address your denial?

8. In what areas of your life are you now beginning to face reality and break the effects of denial?

9. Are you starting to develop a support team? Are you asking for phone numbers in your meetings? List them here or on the inside back cover of this participant's guide!

LESSON 2

Powerless

Principle 1: Realize I'm not God. I admit that I am powerless to control my tendency to do the wrong thing and that my life is unmanageable.

Blessed are the poor in spirit, for theirs is the kingdom of heaven. (Matthew 5:3)

Step 1: We admitted we were powerless over our addictions and compulsive behaviors, that our lives had become unmanageable.

For I know that good itself does not dwell in me, that is, in my sinful nature. For I have the desire to do what is good, but I cannot carry it out. (Romans 7:18)

Think About It

When we accept the first recovery principle and take that first step out of our denial and into reality, we see there are very few things that we really have control over. Once we admit that by ourselves we are powerless we can stop living with the following "serenity robbers," spelled out in the acrostic POWERLESS.

<u>P</u>ride

Ignorance + power + pride = a deadly mixture

Pride brings a person low, but the lowly in spirit gain honor. (Proverbs 29:23)

<u>O</u>nly ifs

Our "only ifs" in life keep us trapped in the fantasyland of rationalization!

There is nothing concealed that will not be disclosed, or hidden that will not be made known. What you have said in the dark will be heard in the daylight, and what you have whispered in the ear in the inner rooms will be proclaimed from the roofs. (Luke 12:2–3)

<u>W</u>orry

Worry steals our peace and doesn't fix our problems.

Therefore do not worry about tomorrow, for tomorrow will worry about itself. Each day has enough trouble of its own. (Matthew 6:34)

<u>E</u>scape

By living in denial we may have escaped into a world of fantasy and unrealistic expectations of ourselves and others.

But everything exposed by the light becomes visible—and everything that is illuminated becomes a light. This is why it is said: "Wake up, sleeper, rise from the dead, and Christ will shine on you." (Ephesians 5:13–14)

Resentments
Resentments act like an emotional cancer if they are allowed to fester and grow.

"In your anger do not sin": Do not let the sun go down while you are still angry, and do not give the devil a foothold. (Ephesians 4:26–27)

Loneliness
In recovery and in Christ, you never have to walk alone.

Keep on loving one another as brothers and sisters. Do not forget to show hospitality to strangers, for by so doing some people have shown hospitality to angels without knowing it. Continue to remember those in prison as if you were together with them in prison, and those who are mistreated as if you yourselves were suffering. (Hebrews 13:1–3)

Emptiness
You know that empty feeling deep inside. The cold wind of hopelessness blows right through it.

The thief comes only to steal and kill and destroy; I have come that they may have life, and have it to the full. (John 10:10)

Selfishness
We often pray: "Our Father which art in heaven; give me, give me, give me."

Whoever tries to keep their life will lose it, and whoever loses their life will preserve it. (Luke 17:33)

Separation
Some people talk about finding God—as if He could ever get lost!

For I am convinced that neither death nor life, neither angels nor demons, neither the present nor the future, nor any powers, neither height nor depth, nor anything else in all creation, will be able to separate us from the love of God that is in Christ Jesus our Lord. (Romans 8:38–39)

Congratulations! In your admission of your powerlessness you have begun the journey of recovery that will allow you to accept the true and only Higher Power's—Jesus Christ's—healing, love, and forgiveness. At this stage in your recovery, you need to stop doing two things:

1. STOP DENYING THE PAIN

You are ready to take your first step in recovery when your pain is greater than your fear.

Have mercy on me, LORD, for I am faint; heal me, LORD, for my bones are in agony. My soul is in deep anguish. How long, LORD, how long? (Psalm 6:2–3)

2. STOP PLAYING GOD

You are unable to do for yourself what you need God to do for you. You are either going to serve God or yourself. You can't serve both.

No one can serve two masters. Either you will hate the one and love the other, or you will be devoted to the one and despise the other. You cannot serve both God and money. (Matthew 6:24)

In addition to stopping certain behaviors, you need to start doing two things:

1. START ADMITTING YOUR POWERLESSNESS

As you work the first principle, you will see that by yourself you do not have the power to change your hurts, hang-ups, and habits.

"With man this is impossible, but with God all things are possible." (Matthew 19:26)

2. START ADMITTING THAT YOUR LIFE HAS BECOME UNMANAGEABLE

You can finally start admitting that some or all areas of your life are out of your control to change.

For troubles without number surround me; my sins have overtaken me, and I cannot see. They are more than the hairs of my head, and my heart fails within me. (Psalm 40:12)

PRINCIPLE 1 PRAYER

Dear God, I can't heal my hurts, hang-ups, and habits by just saying that they are not there. Help me! Parts of my life, or all of my life, are out of control. I now know that I cannot "fix" myself. It seems the harder that I try to do the right thing the more I struggle. Lord, I want to step out of my denial into the truth. I pray for You to show me the way. In Your Son's name I pray, Amen.

Note: Before you begin "Write About It," read the "Prayer for Serenity" on page xiii and read the Principle 1 verses on page 15.

Write About It

1. List some of the ways that your pride has stopped you from asking for and getting the help you need to overcome your hurts, hang-ups, and habits.

2. What in your past has caused you to have the "if onlys"?
    "If only" I had stopped _____ years ago. "If only" _____ hadn't left me.

3. Instead of worrying about things that we cannot control, we need to focus on what God can do in our lives. What are you worrying about? Why?

4. In what ways have you tried to escape your past pain? Be specific.

5. How has holding on to your anger and your resentments affected you?

6. How has denial isolated you from your important relationships?

7. Describe the emptiness you feel and some new ways you are finding to fill it.

8. In what areas of your life have you been selfish?

9. Separation from God can feel very real, but it is never permanent. What can you do to get closer to God?

PRINCIPLE 1 VERSES

But you, Lord, do not be far from me. You are my strength; come quickly to help me. (Psalm 22:19)

Lord, do not rebuke me in your anger or discipline me in your wrath. Have mercy on me, Lord, for I am faint; heal me, Lord, for my bones are in agony. My soul is in deep anguish. How long, Lord, how long? (Psalm 6:1–3)

I do not understand what I do. For what I want to do I do not do, but what I hate I do. And if I do what I do not want to do, I agree that the law is good. As it is, it is no longer I myself who do it, but it is sin living in me. (Romans 7:15–17)

There is a way that appears to be right, but in the end it leads to death. (Proverbs 14:12)

My days have passed, my plans are shattered. Yet the desires of my heart turn night into day; in the face of the darkness light is near. (Job 17:11–12)

I am worn out from my groaning. All night long I flood my bed with weeping and drench my couch with tears. My eyes grow weak with sorrow; they fail because of all my foes. (Psalm 6:6–7)

Indeed, we felt we had received the sentence of death. But this happened that we might not rely on ourselves but on God, who raises the dead. (2 Corinthians 1:9)

LESSON 3

Hope

Principle 2: Earnestly believe that God exists, that I matter to Him, and that He has the power to help me recover.

Blessed are those who mourn, for they will be comforted. (Matthew 5:4)

Step 2: We came to believe that a power greater than ourselves could restore us to sanity.

For it is God who works in you to will and to act in order to fulfill his good purpose. (Philippians 2:13)

Think About It

And without faith it is impossible to please God, because anyone who comes to him must believe that he exists and that he rewards those who earnestly seek him. (Hebrews 11:6)

In the first principle, we admitted we were powerless. Now in the second principle, we come to believe God exists, that we are important to Him, and that we are able to receive God's power to help us recover. It's in the second step we find HOPE!

Higher Power

Our Higher Power has a name: Jesus Christ! Jesus desires a hands-on, day-to-day, moment-to-moment relationship with us. He can do for us what we have never been able to do for ourselves.

Oh, the depth of the riches of the wisdom and knowledge of God! How unsearchable his judgments, and his paths beyond tracing out! "Who has known the mind of the Lord? Or who has been his counselor?" "Who has ever given to God, that God should repay them?" For from him and through him and for him are all things. To him be the glory forever! Amen. (Romans 11:33–36)

But he said to me, "My grace is sufficient for you, for my power is made perfect in weakness." Therefore I will boast all the more gladly about my weaknesses, so that Christ's power may rest on me. (2 Corinthians 12:9)

Openness to change

Throughout our lives, we will continue to encounter hurts and trials that we are powerless to change. With God's help, we need to be open to allow those trials to change us. To make us better, not bitter.

You were taught, with regard to your former way of life, to put off your old self, which is being corrupted by its deceitful desires; to be made new in the attitude of your minds; and to put on the new self, created to be like God in true righteousness and holiness. (Ephesians 4:22–24)

Power to change

In the past, we have wanted to change and were unable to do so. We could not free ourselves from our hurts, hang-ups, or habits. In Principle 2, we come to understand that God's power can change us and our situation.

I can do all this through him who gives me strength. (Philippians 4:13)

Guide me in your truth and teach me, for you are God my Savior, and my hope is in you all day long. (Psalm 25:5)

Expect to change

Remember you are only at the second principle. Don't quit before the miracle happens! With God's help, the changes that you have longed for are just *steps* away.

In all my prayers for all of you, I always pray with joy because of your partnership in the gospel from the first day until now, being confident of this, that he who began a good work in you will carry it on to completion until the day of Christ Jesus. (Philippians 1:4–6)

How do we find hope? By faith in our Higher Power, Jesus Christ.

Now faith is confidence in what we hope for and assurance about what we do not see. (Hebrews 11:1)

Write About It

1. Before taking this step, where were you trying to find hope?

2. What do you believe about God? What are some of His characteristics?

3. How are your feelings for your heavenly Father and your earthly father alike? How do they differ?

4. How can your relationship with your Higher Power, Jesus Christ, help you step out of your denial and face reality?

5. In what areas of your life are you now ready to let God help you?

6. What things are you ready to change in your life? Where can you get the power to change them?

LESSON 4

Sanity

Principle 2: Earnestly believe that God exists, that I matter to Him, and that He has the power to help me recover.

Blessed are those who mourn, for they will be comforted. (Matthew 5:4)

Step 2: We came to believe that a power greater than ourselves could restore us to sanity.

For it is God who works in you to will and to act in order to fulfill his good purpose. (Philippians 2:13)

Think About It

Insanity has been described as "doing the same thing over and over again, expecting a different result each time."

Sanity has been defined as "wholeness of mind; making decisions based on the truth."

The following are some of the gifts we will receive when we believe that our Higher Power, Jesus Christ, has the power and will restore us to SANITY!

Strength

Jesus gives us strength to face the fears that in the past have caused us to fight, flee, or freeze.

God is our refuge and strength, an ever-present help in trouble. Therefore we will not fear, though the earth give way and the mountains fall into the heart of the sea, though its waters roar and foam and the mountains quake with their surging. (Psalm 46:1–3)

My flesh and my heart may fail, but God is the strength of my heart and my portion forever. (Psalm 73:26)

Acceptance

We learn to have realistic expectations of ourselves and others.

May the God who gives endurance and encouragement give you the same attitude of mind toward each other that Christ Jesus had, so that with one mind and one voice you may glorify the God and Father of our Lord Jesus Christ. Accept one another, then, just as Christ accepted you, in order to bring praise to God. (Romans 15:5–7)

New life

We discover that we have an opportunity for a second chance! We can find healing from our past, and do not have to live by our old ways any longer.

Therefore, if anyone is in Christ, the new creation has come: The old has gone, the new is here! (2 Corinthians 5:17)

SANITY

Integrity
We begin to follow through on our promises. Others start trusting what we say.

It gave me great joy when some believers came and testified about your faithfulness to the truth, telling how you continue to walk in it. I have no greater joy than to hear that my children are walking in the truth. (3 John 3–4)

Trust
We begin to trust relationships with others and our Higher Power, Jesus Christ!

Trust in the LORD with all your heart and lean not on your own understanding; in all your ways submit to him, and he will make your paths straight. (Proverbs 3:5–6)

Your Higher Power, Jesus Christ, loves you just the way you are!
No matter what you have done in the past, God wants to forgive it.

While we were still sinners, Christ died for us. (Romans 5:8)

No matter what shape your life is in today, together God and you can handle it!

And God is faithful; he will not let you be tempted beyond what you can bear. But when you are tempted, he will also provide a way out. (1 Corinthians 10:13)

"I will exalt you, LORD, for you lifted me out of the depths and did not let my enemies gloat over me. LORD my God, I called to you for help, and you healed me." (Psalm 30:1–2)

"The righteous cry out, and the LORD hears them; he delivers them from all their troubles. The LORD is close to the brokenhearted and saves those who are crushed in spirit." (Psalm 34:17–18)

And if you take action to complete the next principle, your future will be blessed and secure!

Therefore do not worry about tomorrow, for tomorrow will worry about itself. Each day has enough trouble of its own. (Matthew 6:34)

THE JOURNEY BEGINS

PRINCIPLE 2 PRAYER

Dear God, I have tried to "fix" and "control" my life's hurts, hang-ups, or habits all by myself. I admit that, by myself, I am powerless to change. I need to begin to believe and receive Your power to help me recover. You loved me enough to send Your Son to the cross to die for my sins. Help me be open to the hope that I can only find in Him. Please help me to start living my life one day at a time. In Jesus' name I pray, Amen.

Write About It

1. What things have you been doing over and over again, expecting a different result each time (insanity)?

2. What is your definition of sanity?

3. How have your past expectations of yourself or others been unrealistic? Give examples.

4. In the past, how has trusting only in your own feelings and emotions gotten you in trouble?

5. How can your Higher Power, Jesus Christ, help restore you to make sane decisions? How do you get a second chance?

6. What areas of your life are you ready to release control of and hand over to God? Be specific.

PRINCIPLE 2 VERSES

Remember that at that time you were separate from Christ, excluded from citizenship in Israel and foreigners to the covenants of the promise, without hope and without God in the world. But now in Christ Jesus you who once were far away have been brought near by the blood of Christ. (Ephesians 2:12–13)

But we have this treasure in jars of clay to show that this all-surpassing power is from God and not from us. We are hard pressed on every side, but not crushed; perplexed, but not in despair; persecuted, but not abandoned; struck down, but not destroyed. (2 Corinthians 4:7–9)

To them God has chosen to make known among the Gentiles the glorious riches of this mystery, which is Christ in you, the hope of glory. (Colossians 1:27)

Do not conform to the pattern of this world, but be transformed by the renewing of your mind. Then you will be able to test and approve what God's will is—his good, pleasing and perfect will. (Romans 12:2)

THE JOURNEY BEGINS

The righteous cry out, and the LORD hears them; he delivers them from all their troubles. The LORD is close to the brokenhearted and saves those who are crushed in spirit. (Psalm 34:17–18)

As for me, I call to God, and the LORD saves me. Evening, morning and noon I cry out in distress, and he hears my voice. (Psalm 55:16–17)

LESSON 5

Turn

Principle 3: Consciously choose to commit all my life and will to Christ's care and control.

Blessed are the meek, for they will inherit the earth. (Matthew 5:5)

Step 3: We made a decision to turn our lives and our wills over to the care of God.

Therefore, I urge you, brothers and sisters, in view of God's mercy, to offer your bodies as a living sacrifice, holy and pleasing to God—this is your true and proper worship. (Romans 12:1)

Think About It

How do you TURN your life over to the one and only Higher Power, Jesus Christ?

Trust

Deciding to turn your life and your will over to God requires only trust. Trust is putting the faith you found in Principle 2 into action.

If you declare with your mouth, "Jesus is Lord," and believe in your heart that God raised him from the dead, you will be saved. (Romans 10:9)

Understand

Relying solely on your own understanding got you into recovery in the first place! After you make the decision to ask Jesus into your life, you need to begin to seek His will for your life in all your decisions.

Trust in the LORD with all your heart and lean not on your own understanding; in all your ways submit to him, and he will make your paths straight. (Proverbs 3:5–6)

Repent

To truly repent, you must not only *turn away* from your sins, but *turn toward* God. Repentance allows you to enjoy the freedom of your loving relationship with God.

"The time has come," he said. "The kingdom of God has come near. Repent and believe the good news!" (Mark 1:15)

Do not conform to the pattern of this world, but be transformed by the renewing of your mind. Then you will be able to test and approve what God's will is—his good, pleasing and perfect will. (Romans 12:2)

New life

After you ask Jesus into your heart, you will have a new life! You will no longer be bound to your old sin nature. God has declared you NOT GUILTY, and you no longer have to live under the power of sin!

Therefore, there is now no condemnation for those who are in Christ Jesus, because through Christ Jesus the law of the Spirit who gives life has set you free from the law of sin and death. (Romans 8:1–2)

Therefore, if anyone is in Christ, the new creation has come: The old has gone, the new is here! (2 Corinthians 5:17)

We will work on the "how tos" of TURNING our life and will over to God in Lesson 6. But do not forget this key point:

Turning your life over to Christ is a once-in-a-lifetime commitment!
Turning your will over to Him requires a daily recommitment!
Pray the following prayer daily.

PRINCIPLE 3 PRAYER

Dear God, I have tried to do it all by myself, on my own power, and I have failed. Today, I want to turn my life over to You. I ask You to be my Lord and my Savior. You are the One and only Higher Power! I ask that You help me start to think less about me and my will. I want to daily turn my will over to You, to daily seek Your direction and wisdom for my life. Please continue to help me overcome my hurts, hang-ups, and habits and may that victory over them help others as they see Your power at work in changing my life. Help me to do Your will always. In Jesus' name I pray, Amen.

Write About It

1. What is stopping you from asking Jesus Christ into your heart as your Lord and Savior? (If you have already asked Christ into your life, describe your experience.)

2. How has relying on your "own understanding" caused problems in your life? Be specific.

3. What does "repent" mean to you? What do you need to repent of?

4. What does the declaration of "no condemnation" found in Romans 8:1–2 mean to you?

5. When you turn your life over to your Higher Power, Jesus Christ, you have a new life (see 2 Corinthians 5:17). What does that "new life" mean to you?

6. What does the Principle 3 prayer mean to you?

LESSON 6

Action

Principle 3: Consciously choose to commit all my life and will to Christ's care and control.

Blessed are the meek, for they will inherit the earth. (Matthew 5:5)

Step 3: We made a decision to turn our lives and our wills over to the care of God.

Therefore, I urge you, brothers and sisters, in view of God's mercy, to offer your bodies as a living sacrifice, holy and pleasing to God—this is your true and proper worship. (Romans 12:1)

Think About It

Even after taking the first two steps we can still be stuck in the cycle of failure: shame → anger → fear → depression!

How do we get "unstuck"? How do we get past the barriers of pride, fear, guilt, worry, and doubt that keep us from taking this step?

The answer is *we need to take ACTION!*

Accept Jesus Christ as your Higher Power and Savior!

Make the decision to ask Jesus into your heart. Now is the time to commit your life, to establish that personal relationship with Jesus that He so desires.

If you declare with your mouth, "Jesus is Lord," and believe in your heart that God raised him from the dead, you will be saved. (Romans 10:9)

Commit to seek and follow HIS will!

We need to change our definition of willpower: Willpower is the willingness to accept God's power. We see that there is no room for God if we are full of ourselves.

Teach me to do your will, for you are my God; may your good Spirit lead me on level ground. (Psalm 143:10)

Turn it over

"Let go; let God!" Turn over all the big things and the little things in your life to your Higher Power. Jesus Christ wants a relationship with *ALL* of you. What burdens are you carrying that you want to *TURN OVER* to God?

"Come to me, all you who are weary and burdened, and I will give you rest. Take my yoke upon you and learn from me, for I am gentle and humble in heart, and you will find rest for your souls. For my yoke is easy and my burden is light." (Matthew 11:28–30)

ACTION

It's only the beginning

In the third principle we make only the initial decision, the commitment to seek and follow God's will. Our walk with our Higher Power, Jesus Christ, begins with this decision and is followed by a lifelong process of growing as a Christian.

In all my prayers for all of you, I always pray with joy because of your partnership in the gospel from the first day until now, being confident of this, that he who began a good work in you will carry it on to completion until the day of Christ Jesus. (Philippians 1:4–6)

One day at a time

Recovery happens one day at a time. If we remain stuck in the yesterday or constantly worry about tomorrow, we will waste the precious time of the present. We can only change our hurts, hang-ups, and habits in the present.

Therefore do not worry about tomorrow, for tomorrow will worry about itself. Each day has enough trouble of its own. (Matthew 6:34)

Next: How do I ask Christ into my life?

Ask yourself the following four questions (see box), and if you answer yes to all of them, pray the prayer that follows them. That's it. That's all you have to do!

How to Establish a "Spiritual Base" for My Life

By Pastor Rick Warren

Do I . . .

Believe Jesus Christ died on the cross for me and showed He was God by coming back to life?
(1 Corinthians 15:2–4)

Do I . . .

Accept God's free forgiveness for my sins?
(Romans 3:22)

Do I . . .

Switch to God's plan for my life?
(Mark 1:16–18; Romans 12:2)

Do I . . .

Express my desire to Christ to be the director of my life?
(Romans 10:9)

Dear God, I believe you sent Your Son, Jesus, to die for my sins so I can be forgiven. I'm sorry for my sins and I want to live the rest of my life the way you want me to. Please put Your Spirit in my life to direct me. Amen.

ACTION

Write About It

1. What differences have you noticed in your life now that you have accepted Jesus Christ as your Higher Power?

2. How has your definition of willpower changed since you have been in recovery?

3. What have you been able to turn over to God?

4. What do you fear turning over to His care?

5. What is keeping you from turning them over?

6. What does the phrase "live one day at a time" mean to you?

7. What is a major concern in your life?

8. What's stopping you from turning it over to your Higher Power, Jesus Christ?

PRINCIPLE 3 VERSES

If you declare with your mouth, "Jesus is Lord," and believe in your heart that God raised him from the dead, you will be saved. (Romans 10:9)

He replied, "Because you have so little faith. Truly I tell you, if you have faith as small as a mustard seed, you can say to this mountain, 'Move from here to there,' and it will move. Nothing will be impossible for you." (Matthew 17:20)

"Come to me, all you who are weary and burdened, and I will give you rest. Take my yoke upon you and learn from me, for I am gentle and humble in heart, and you will find rest for your souls. For my yoke is easy and my burden is light." (Matthew 11:28–30)

Commit your way to the Lord; trust in him and he will do this." (Psalm 37:5)

Guide me in your truth and teach me, for you are God my Savior, and my hope is in you all day long. (Psalm 25:5)

Indeed, we felt we had received the sentence of death. But this happened that we might not rely on ourselves but on God, who raises the dead. (2 Corinthians 1:9)

Teach me to do your will, for you are my God; may your good Spirit lead me on level ground. (Psalm 143:10)

Trust in the Lord with all your heart and lean not on your own understanding; in all your ways submit to him, and he will make your paths straight. (Proverbs 3:5–6)

Congratulations!

Congratulations! This is a time to reflect and celebrate with one another the accomplishment of completing the first book! Before you go onto Volume 2, your group might want to spend one meeting sharing some of the differences you are experiencing compared to starting this journey. If you live in the same area, getting together for a meal or coffee to celebrate your accomplishment is a fun way to continue the closeness you are developing with the group.

Your Next Step

In Principle 1 you faced your denial and admitted that by yourself you were powerless to manage your addictive or compulsive behavior.

For I know that good itself does not dwell in me, that is, in my sinful nature. For I have the desire to do what is good, but I cannot carry it out. (Romans 7:18)

In Principle 2 you found the hope that God could and would restore you to sanity, and that only He could provide the power for you to recover.

Therefore, my dear friends, as you have always obeyed—not only in my presence, but now much more in my absence—continue to work out your salvation with fear and trembling, for it is God who works in you to will and to act in order to fulfill his good purpose. (Philippians 2:12–13)

And finally, in Principle 3, you were able to take the action, to make the decision to turn your life and your will over to God's care and direction.

Therefore, I urge you, brothers and sisters, in view of God's mercy, to offer your bodies as a living sacrifice, holy and pleasing to God—this is your true and proper worship. Do not conform to the pattern of this world, but be transformed by the renewing of your mind. Then you will be able to test and approve what God's will is—his good, pleasing and perfect will. (Romans 12:1–2)

Now, you are ready to take the next step in your journey on the "Road to Recovery." Volume 2 deals with facing your past—the good and the bad. Principle 4 can be difficult, but remember you're not going to go through it alone. Your Higher Power, Jesus Christ, and others that He has placed alongside you on your "Road to Recovery" will be with you every step of the way.

Taking an Honest Spiritual Inventory

THE JOURNEY BEGINS

Introduction

You have completed the first three principles to the best of your ability: You have "gotten right with God." Now as you prepare to work Principle 4, you begin the journey of "getting right with yourself" (Principles 4–5).

After each lesson, there is an exercise for you to complete. Answer each question to the best of your ability. Don't worry about what you think the answer *should* be. Pray and then write down the answer from your heart. Remember John 8:32: "Then you will know the truth, and the truth will set you free."

An important word of caution: Do not begin this principle without a sponsor or a strong accountability partner (these are explained in Lesson 7)! You need someone you trust to help keep you balanced during this step, not to do the work for you. Nobody can do that except you. But you need encouragement from someone who will support your progress and keep you accountable. That's what this program is all about.

After you have completed the exercise, share it with someone that you trust. Your group, an accountability partner, your sponsor or a close friend in recovery are all safe choices. You do not recover from your hurts, hang-ups, and habits from just attending recovery meetings. You must work and live the principles!

In His steps,
John Baker

Lesson 7

Sponsor

Principle 4: Openly examine and confess my hurts, hang-ups, and habits to myself, to God, and to someone I trust.

Blessed are the pure in heart, for they will see God. (Matthew 5:8)

Step 4: We made a searching and fearless moral inventory of ourselves.

Let us examine our ways and test them, and let us return to the LORD. (Lamentations 3:40)

Think About It

You've heard the word "sponsor" for a few weeks now. I'm sure you have at least a vague idea of what a sponsor is, but maybe you're wondering why you even need one.

Why do I need a sponsor and/or an accountability partner?

There are three reasons why having a sponsor and/or accountability partner is vital. **Having a sponsor and/or accountability partner is biblical.**

Two are better than one, because they have a good return for their labor: If either of them falls down, one can help the other up. But pity anyone who falls and has no one to help them up. Also, if two lie down together, they will keep warm. But how can one keep warm alone? Though one may be overpowered, two can defend themselves. A cord of three strands is not quickly broken. (Ecclesiastes 4:9–12)

As iron sharpens iron, so one person sharpens another. (Proverbs 27:17)

Having a sponsor and/or accountability partner is a key part of your recovery program. Your recovery program has four key elements to success:

- Maintain your **relationship** with Jesus Christ, through prayer, meditation, and studying His Word.
- To the best of your ability, maintain your honest view of reality as you work each principle. The best way to ensure this is to have a sponsor and develop a strong accountability support team.
- Make recovery group **meetings** a priority in your schedule. Knowing that a sponsor or accountability partner will be there to greet you or notice that you're not there is an added incentive to attend.
- Get involved in **service**, which includes serving as a sponsor (after you have completed all eight principles) or accountability partner.

Having a sponsor and/or an accountability partner is the best guard against relapse. By providing feedback to keep you on track, a sponsor and/or accountability partner can see your old dysfunctional hurts, hang-ups, and habits beginning to return, and point them out to you quickly. He or she can confront you with truth and love without placing shame or guilt.

What are the qualities of a sponsor?

The purposes of a person's heart are deep waters, but one who has insight draws them out. (Proverbs 20:5)

When you are selecting a possible sponsor, look for the following qualities:

1. Does their walk match their talk? Are they living by the eight principles?
2. Do they have a growing relationship with Jesus Christ?
3. Do they express the desire to help others on the "road to recovery"?
4. Do they show compassion, care, and hope, but not pity?
5. Are they a good listener?
6. Are they strong enough to confront your denial or procrastination?
7. Do they offer suggestions?
8. Can they share their own current struggles with others?

What is the role of a sponsor?

1. Most important, they continually point you to Jesus as your Higher Power. They do not work the steps for you!
2. They can be there to discuss issues in detail that are too personal or would take too much time in a meeting.
3. They are available in times of crisis or potential relapse.
4. They serve as a sounding board by providing an objective point of view.
5. They are there to encourage you to work the principles at your own speed.
6. They attempt to model the lifestyle resulting from working the eight principles.
7. A sponsor can resign or can be fired.

How do I find a sponsor and/or an accountability partner?

First, your sponsor or accountability partner MUST be of the same gender as you. After you have narrowed the field down with that requirement, listen to people share. Do you relate to or resonate with what is spoken? Ask others in your group to go out for coffee after the meeting. Get to know the person before you ask them to be your sponsor or accountability partner!

If you ask someone to be your sponsor or accountability partner and that person says no, do not take it as a personal rejection. Ask someone else. You can even ask for a "temporary" sponsor or accountability partner.

Ask God to lead you to the sponsor and/or accountability partner of His choosing. He already has someone in mind for you.

What is the difference between a sponsor and an accountability partner?

A sponsor is someone who has worked through the eight principles and 12 Steps. The main goal of this relationship is to choose someone to guide you through the program.

An accountability partner is someone you ask to hold you accountable for certain areas of your recovery or issues, such as meeting attendance, journaling, and so forth. This person can be at the same level of recovery as you are, behind you, or ahead of you. The main goal of this relationship is to encourage one another. While you only have one sponsor at a time, you can have many accountability partners.

The accountability partner or group acts as the "team," whereas the sponsor's role is that of a "coach."

NOTE: Sometimes it can be hard to find a sponsor. If you're having trouble, lean into your accountability partners, and do NOT give up working your recovery journey. We recommend you continue searching for a sponsor, but also continue working the steps with an accountability partner.

SPONSOR

Write About It

1. Why is it important for you to have a support team?

2. What qualities are you looking for in a sponsor and/or accountability partner?

3. How have you attempted to find a sponsor and/or accountability partner?

4. What are some new places and ways you can try to find a sponsor and/or accountability partner?

5. What is the difference between a sponsor and an accountability partner?

6. List the names and phone numbers of possible sponsors or accountability partners. These should be individuals you have met on your "Road to Recovery" who have touched you in the sharing of their experiences, strengths, and hopes.

LESSON 8

Moral

Principle 4: Openly examine and confess my hurts, hang-ups, and habits to myself, to God, and to someone I trust.

Blessed are the pure in heart, for they will see God. (Matthew 5:8)

Step 4: We made a searching and fearless moral inventory of ourselves.

Let us examine our ways and test them, and let us return to the Lord. (Lamentations 3:40)

An important word of caution: Do not begin this principle without a sponsor or a strong accountability partner (these are explained in Lesson 7)! You need someone you trust to help keep you balanced during this step, not to do the work for you. Nobody can do that except you. But you need encouragement from someone who will support your progress and hold you accountable. That's what this program is all about.

Think About It

In this principle, you need to list (inventory) all the significant events—good and bad—in your life. You need to be as honest as you can be to allow God to show you how you've been hurt, how you've hurt others, and how that has affected you and others.. The acrostic for MORAL shows you how to begin.

<u>M</u>ake time

Set aside a special time to begin your inventory. Schedule an appointment with yourself. Set aside a day or a weekend to get alone with God! Clear your mind of the present hassles of daily life.

He says, "Be still, and know that I am God; I will be exalted among the nations, I will be exalted in the earth." (Psalm 46:10)

<u>O</u>pen

Open your heart and your mind to allow the feelings that the pain of the past has blocked or caused you to deny. Try to "wake up" your feelings! Ask yourself, "How have I been hurt? What do I feel guilty about? Who do I resent? What do I fear? Am I trapped in self-pity? Am I trapped in false beliefs about myself, God, or others?"

"Therefore I will not keep silent; I will speak out in the anguish of my spirit, I will complain in the bitterness of my soul." (Job 7:11)

<u>R</u>ely

Rely on Jesus, your Higher Power, to give you the courage and strength this exercise requires.

Love the LORD, all his faithful people! The LORD preserves those who are true to him, but the proud he pays back in full. Be strong and take heart, all you who hope in the LORD. (Psalm 31:23–24)

Analyze

Analyze your past honestly. To do a "searching and fearless moral inventory," you need to step out of your denial and be honest—that's what moral means; honest.

This step requires looking through your denial of the past into the truth!

The human spirit is the lamp of the LORD that sheds light on one's inmost being.
(Proverbs 20:27)

List

List both the good and the bad. Keep your inventory balanced! If you just look at all the bad things of your past, you will distort your inventory and open yourself to unnecessary pain.

Let us examine our ways and test them. (Lamentations 3:40)

The verse doesn't say, "Examine only your bad, negative ways." You need to honestly focus on how you've been hurt, who you have hurt, the good things you have done, as well as the good things that have been done to you!

As you compile your inventory, you will find that you have done some harmful things to yourself and others. No one's inventory (life) is flawless. We have all "missed the mark" in some area of our lives. In recovery we are not to dwell on the past, but we need to understand it so we can begin to allow God to change us. Jesus told us, "The thief comes only to steal and kill and destroy; I have come that they may have life, and have it to the full" (John 10:10).

PRINCIPLE 4 PRAYER

Dear God, You know my past, all the good and the bad things. Both the things I've done, and the things that have been done to me. In this step, I ask that You give me the strength and the courage to list those things so that I can "come clean" and face them and the truth. Please help me reach out to others You have placed along my "road to recovery." Thank You for providing them to help me keep balanced as I do my inventory. In Christ's name I pray, Amen.

Write About It

1. Where will you go for quiet time to begin your inventory?

2. What date have you set aside to start? What time?

3. What are your fears as you begin your inventory? Why?

4. What can you do to help you "wake up" your feelings?

5. How do you attempt to turn over your will to God's care on a daily basis?

6. List the things you have used to block the pain of your past.

MORAL

7. What have you done to step out of your denial?

8. How can you continue to find new ways out of your denial of the past?

9. Why is it important to do a written inventory?

10. What are some of the good things you have done in the past?

11. What are some of the negative things you have done in the past?

12. Do you have a sponsor or accountability partner to help you keep your inventory balanced?

LESSON 9

Inventory

Principle 4: Openly examine and confess my hurts, hang-ups, and habits to myself, to God, and to someone I trust.

Blessed are the pure in heart, for they will see God. (Matthew 5:8)

Step 4: We made a searching and fearless moral inventory of ourselves.

Let us examine our ways and test them, and let us return to the Lord. (Lamentations 3:40)

Think About It

Now that you have the background information and you've built your accountability team, it's time to start writing your inventory. This lesson will provide you with the tools you need. Getting all of it down helps you to clearly see the connection between the hurts that lead to hang-ups that created habits. You'll discover the root issues that show up as emotional triggers, repeated patterns of behavior, and character defects. You will be amazed by the transformation it brings, and how you will grow in your relationship with Jesus Christ in the process!

How do I start my inventory?

The Celebrate Recovery Inventory is divided into five sections. It will help you keep focused on reality and recall events that you may have repressed. Remember, you are not going through this alone. You are developing your support team to guide you, but even more important, you are growing in your relationship with Jesus Christ!

It will take you more than one page to write out your inventory. You have permission to copy the "Celebrate Recovery Principle 4 Inventory Worksheet" on pages 59 and 60.

Column 1: "Who hurt me?"

In this column, **you list the person or institution who hurt you**. So even though this column is called The Person it can also be institutions or places. For example, you may have resentments, fears, or negative emotions toward an organization like the church, the government, or the medical establishment. Or you may have been dealing with a chronic illness that has built up resentment. While working on this list, go back as far as you can into early childhood. Sometimes, people feel guilty listing their parents or other caregivers, but we've all been raised by imperfect people. We list them to explain and understand our history, not to assign blame. Again, list people, institutions, or places. If you get overwhelmed, back up and take it one event at a time. Pick one or two events that had the most impact on you and your life and start there. Then move on to one or two more. Pray and ask God who or what from your life needs to go in Column 1. He is faithful and will show you. Lamentations 3:22–23 tells us, "Because of the Lord's great love we are not consumed, for his compassions never fail. They are new every morning; great is your faithfulness." We are not alone in this process!

Column 2: "What happened?"

In this column, you are going to **list what happened** when the person or institution hurt you. It is important to be specific about these actions. For example, you might list a parent who always told you to stop crying or told you your feelings didn't matter. Friends may have dismissed your feelings as you went through a divorce. These reflections can be painful, but God is with us every step of the way.

Isaiah 41:10 says, "So do not fear, for I am with you; do not be dismayed, for I am your God. I will strengthen you and help you; I will uphold you with my righteous right hand." It is imperative to have a sponsor and/or accountability partner supporting you as you work on this inventory. They will be there to support you as you walk through the pain, some or all of this group can be accountability partners. If you do not have one, keep looking! Your step study group is also working through the same process You can begin to build relationships with them. They will be there to support you as you walk through the pain.

Column 3: "How did you feel?"

In this column, you will **list how did this action make you feel**. It is important to acknowledge our emotions. These emotions affect what we believe, which in turn. directly affects our behaviors, or habits. Many of us were taught to repress our emotions. If we cannot express how we feel, or how we were hurt, then we cannot heal. Denying our pain and emotions does not make them go away. They store up in our body and make us hurt until we feel them. Try to list two or three emotions in this column. Since so many of us were taught to disconnect from our emotions from an early age, this can be very difficult. It can help to have an emotions list on hand as you work on your inventory.

Trust in him at all times, you people; pour out our hearts to him, for God is our refuge. (Psalm 62:8)

Column 4: "What was the damage?"

In this column, you are going to **list what was the damage**. This includes any beliefs you might have developed as a result. Remember, how you've been hurt directly affects what you think or believe about yourself, others, or God. These beliefs are our hang-ups. For example, a belief system could be that your emotions make you a burden, or that you are unworthy of love. How did your worldview change? Did you develop mistrust for a group of people based on this particular event? Or is there a pattern of broken relationships, slander, loss of physical safety, financial loss or damaged intimacy from abusive relationships?

No matter how you have been hurt, no matter how lost you may feel, God wants to comfort you and restore you. Remember Ezekiel 34:16: "I will search for the lost and bring back the strays. I will bind up the injured and strengthen the weak, but the sleek and the strong I will destroy. I will shepherd the flock with justice."

Column 5: "What was/What is my part?"

Now it's time to see what part you have played. So far, in Columns 1-4 you have explored how you have been hurt and the impact that pain has had on your life. This is the column where we stop looking outward and we start looking inward. There are two pitfalls to avoid here, one, blaming everyone else for your behaviors and habits and taking no responsibility for your actions, and two, believing that none of the first four columns have had any impact on your choices or formed your coping mechanisms.

Ask yourself, **"What was/what is my part?"** For example, do you try to control others in an attempt to feel safe? Or do you drink, shop, or go online too much in an attempt to escape pain in your life? Also ask yourself, "Did I have a part in the action that hurt me?" If so, write out what your part was.

List all the people whom you have hurt and how you have hurt them. "Search me, God, and know my heart; test me and know my anxious thoughts. See if there is any offensive way in me, and lead me in the way everlasting" (Psalm 139:23–24).

Please note: If you have been in an abusive relationship, especially as a small child, you can find great freedom in this part of the inventory. You see that you had **NO** part, **NO** responsibility for the cause of the resentment. By simply writing the words "none" or "not guilty" in column 5, you can begin to be free from the misplaced shame and guilt you have carried with you.

Celebrate Recovery has rewritten Step 4 for those who have been sexually or physically abused:

Made a searching and fearless moral inventory of ourselves, realizing all wrongs can be forgiven. Renounce the lie that the abuse was our fault.

More tools

1. Memorize Isaiah 1:18: "'Come now, let us settle the matter,' says the Lord. 'Though your sins are like scarlet, they shall be as white as snow; though they are red as crimson, they shall be like wool.'"
2. Read the Principle 4 "Balancing the Scale" verses on page 58.
3. Keep your inventory balanced. List both the good and the bad! This is very important! As God reveals the good things that you have done in the past, or are doing in the present, list them on the reverse side of your copies of the "Celebrate Recovery Principle 4 Inventory Worksheet."
4. Continue to develop your support team.
5. Pray continuously.

PRINCIPLE 4 VERSES

Balancing the Scale

Emotion	Positive Scripture
Helpless	*Therefore, my dear friends, as you have always obeyed—not only in my presence, but now much more in my absence—continue to work out your salvation with fear and trembling, for it is God who works in you to will and to act in order to fulfill his good purpose. (Philippians 2:12–13)*
Shame	*Therefore, if anyone is in Christ, the new creation has come: The old has gone, the new is here! (2 Corinthians 5:17)*
Jealousy	*"And my God will meet all your needs according to the riches of his glory in Christ Jesus." (Philippians 4:19)*
Lonely	*So do not fear, for I am with you; do not be dismayed, for I am your God. I will strengthen you and help you; I will uphold you with my righteous right hand. (Isaiah 41:10)*
Overwhelmed	*The Lord is a refuge for the oppressed, a stronghold in times of trouble. (Psalm 9:9)*
Fear, Doubt	*Have I not commanded you? Be strong and courageous. Do not be afraid; do not be discouraged, for the Lord your God will be with you wherever you go. (Joshua 1:9)*
Melancholy, Apathy	*The Lord has done it this very day; let us rejoice today and be glad. (Psalm 118:24)*
Worry	*Cast all your anxiety on him because he cares for you. (1 Peter 5:7)*

INVENTORY

CELEBRATE RECOVERY

Principle 4 Inventory Worksheet

1. Who hurt me?	2. What happened?	3. How did you feel?
Who is the object of my resentment or fear?	What specific action did that person take that hurt me?	List any emotions that you felt.

THE JOURNEY BEGINS

"Let us examine our ways and test them, and let us return to the Lord." (Lamentations 3:40)

4. What was the damage?	5. What was/What is my part?
What did this action make me believe is true about myself, others, or God? What damage did that action do to my basic social, security, and/or sexual instincts?	As a result of that action, what action did I take? What behaviors did I develop as a way to cope?
	What part am I responsible for?
	Who are the people I have hurt?
	How have I hurt them?

NOTE: Remember to keep your inventory balanced. In each of these areas try to look for positive things you have experienced in the past.

LESSON 10

Spiritual Inventory Part 1

Principle 4: Openly examine and confess my hurts, hang-ups, and habits to myself, to God, and to someone I trust.

Blessed are the pure in heart, for they will see God. (Matthew 5:8)

Step 4: We made a searching and fearless moral inventory of ourselves.

Let us examine our ways and test them, and let us return to the Lord. (Lamentations 3:40)

Think About It

Search me, God, and know my heart; test me and know my anxious thoughts. See if there is any offensive way in me, and lead me in the way everlasting. (Psalm 139:23–24)

The following list will help us explore the first half of some of the things that can prevent God from working effectively in our lives. Reading through it and searching your heart will help you get started on your inventory!

Relationship with others

And forgive us our debts, as we also have forgiven our debtors. And lead us not into temptation, but deliver us from the evil one. (Matthew 6:12–13)

- Who has hurt you?
- Against whom have you been holding a grudge?
- Against whom are you seeking revenge?
- Are you jealous of someone else?

(Note: The people who you name in these areas will go in column 1 of your Celebrate Recovery Principle 4 Inventory Worksheet.)

- Who have you hurt?
- Who have you criticized or gossiped about?
- Have you justified your bad attitude by saying it is "their" fault?

(Note: The people who you name in these areas will go in column 5 of your Celebrate Recovery Principle 4 Inventory Worksheet.)

Priorities in life

But seek first his kingdom and his righteousness, and all these things will be given to you as well. (Matthew 6:33)

SPIRITUAL INVENTORY PART 1

- After accepting Jesus Christ, in what areas of your life are you still not putting God first?
- What in your past is interfering with you doing God's will? Your ambition? Pleasures? Job? Hobbies? Money? Friendships? Personal goals?

Attitude

Get rid of all bitterness, rage and anger, brawling and slander, along with every form of malice. (Ephesians 4:31)

- Have you always complained about your circumstances?
- In what areas of your life are you ungrateful?
- Have you gotten angry and easily blown up at people?
- Have you been sarcastic?
- What in your past is causing you fear or anxiety?

Integrity

Do not lie to each other, since you have taken off your old self with its practices. (Colossians 3:9)

- In what past dealing were you dishonest?
- Have you stolen things?
- Have you exaggerated to make yourself look better?
- In what areas of your past have you used false humility?
- Have you lived one way in front of your Christian friends and another way at home or at work?

Have you memorized Isaiah 1:18 yet?

"Come now, let us settle the matter," says the LORD. "Though your sins are like scarlet, they shall be as white as snow; though they are red as crimson, they shall be like wool."

> **NOTE:** Remember to keep your inventory balanced. In each of these areas try to look for positive things you have experienced in the past.

Write About It

1. Relationship with Others
   - Who has hurt you? (Go as far back as you can.) How did they specifically hurt you?

   - Who are you holding a grudge against? (Seeking revenge?)

   - Who are you jealous of? (Past and present.) Why?

   - Who have you hurt? And how did you hurt them?

   - Who have you been critical of or gossiped about? Why?

   - How have you attempted to place the blame on someone else? (Be specific.)

SPIRITUAL INVENTORY PART 1

- What new healthy relationships have you developed since you have been in recovery?

2. Priorities in Life
    - What areas of your life have you been able to turn over to your Higher Power, Jesus Christ?

    - After acting on Principle 3, in what areas of your life are you still not putting God first? Why not?

    - What in your past is keeping you from seeking and following God's will for your life?

    - Number the following list in order of your personal priorities.
        _____ Career
        _____ Family
        _____ Church
        _____ Christ
        _____ Friendships
        _____ Money
        _____ Ministry

- What are your personal goals for the next ninety days? (Keep it simple!)

3. Attitude
    - What areas in your life are you thankful for?

    - In the past, what things have you been ungrateful over?

    - What causes you to lose your temper?

    - To whom have you been sarcastic to in the past? (Give examples.)

    - What in your past are you still worried about?

SPIRITUAL INVENTORY PART 1

- How has your attitude improved since you have been in recovery?

4 Integrity
- In the past, how have you exaggerated to make yourself look good? (Give examples.)

- Does your walk as a Christian match your talk? Are your actions the same at recovery meetings, church, home, and work?

- In what areas of your past have you used false humility to impress someone?

- Have any of your past business dealings been dishonest? Have you ever stolen things?

- List the ways you have been able to get out of your denial (distorted/dishonest thinking) into God's truth.

LESSON 11

Spiritual Inventory Part 2

Principle 4: Openly examine and confess my hurts, hang-ups, and habits to myself, to God, and to someone I trust.

Blessed are the pure in heart, for they will see God. (Matthew 5:8)

Step 4: We made a searching and fearless moral inventory of ourselves.

Let us examine our ways and test them, and let us return to the Lord. (Lamentations 3:40)

THE JOURNEY BEGINS

Think About It

Search me, God, and know my heart: test me and know my anxious thoughts. See if there is any offensive way in me, and lead me in the way everlasting. (Psalm 139:23–24)

The following list will help us explore the second half of some of the things that can prevent God from working effectively in our lives. Reading through it and searching your heart will help you get started on your inventory!

Your mind

Do not conform to the pattern of this world, but be transformed by the renewing of your mind. Then you will be able to test and approve what God's will is—his good, pleasing and perfect will. (Romans 12:2)

- How have you guarded your mind in the past? Denial?
- In what ways has your emotional and/or mental health been harmed by others?
- Have you filled your mind with hurtful and unhealthy movies, television programs, internet sites, magazines, or books?
- Have you failed to concentrate on the positive truths of the Bible?

Your body

Do you not know that your bodies are temples of the Holy Spirit, who is in you, whom you have received from God? You are not your own; you were bought at a price. Therefore honor God with your bodies. (1 Corinthians 6:19–20)

- In what ways in the past have you mistreated your body?
- In what ways has your body been harmed by others?
- Have you abused alcohol and drugs? Food? Sex?
- What past activities or habits caused harm to your physical health?

SPIRITUAL INVENTORY PART 2

Your family

See what great love the Father has lavished on us, that we should be called children of God! And that is what we are! The reason the world does not know us is that it did not know him. (1 John 3:1)

- In the past, has anyone in your family mistreated you?
- Have you mistreated anyone in your family?
- Who in your family do you have a resentment against?
- To whom do you owe amends?
- What is the family secret that you have been denying?

Your church

And let us consider how we may spur one another on toward love and good deeds, not giving up meeting together, as some are in the habit of doing, but encouraging one another—and all the more as you see the Day approaching. (Hebrews 10:24–25)

- Have you been faithful to your church in the past?
- How have you been hurt by the church?
- Have you been critical rather than active?
- In the past have you discouraged your family's support of their church?
- What in your past has kept you inactive in the church?

As you continue your inventory, commit Psalm 139:23–24 to memory and use it as a prayer:

Search me, God, and know my heart; test me and know my anxious thoughts. See if there is any offensive way in me, and lead me in the way everlasting.

> **NOTE**: Remember to keep your inventory balanced. In each of these areas try to look for positive things you have experienced in the past.

Write About It

1. Your Mind
   - Since accepting Christ as your Higher Power, how has God transformed your mind (Romans 12:2)? What worldly standards have you given up?

   - How have you used denial to attempt to guard your mind?

   - In what ways has your emotional and/or mental health been harmed by others?

   - Have you filled or are you filling your mind with hurtful and unhealthy movies, television programs, Internet sites, magazines, or books?

   - How have you failed to concentrate on the positive truths of the Bible? (Be specific.)

SPIRITUAL INVENTORY PART 2

2. Your Body
   - What past activities or habits caused harm to your physical health?

   - In what ways has your body been harmed by others?

   - In what ways have you mistreated your body?

   - If you have abused alcohol, drugs, foods, or sex, how did they negatively affect your body?

   - What have you done to restore God's temple?

3. Your Family
   - In the past, has anyone in your family hurt you verbally, emotionally, or physically?

THE JOURNEY BEGINS

- Have you mistreated anyone in your family verbally, emotionally, or physically?

- Who in your family do you hold a resentment against? Why?

- Can you think of anyone to whom you owe amends? Why? (Don't worry about actually making them now! That's Principle 6.)

- What is the "family secret" that you have kept denying?

- How have relationships improved since you have been in recovery? (Be specific.)

4. Your Church
    - How would you rate your past participation in your church?
        _____Very involved
        _____Semiactive member
        _____Sideline member
        _____Attender
        _____Went only on holidays
        _____Never attended

SPIRITUAL INVENTORY PART 2

- Prior to your recovery, what was your main reason for going to church?

- Have you ever been hurt by the church?

- Have you ever tried to discourage any family members from church involvement? How? Why?

- How has your commitment to your church increased since starting your recovery? (Give examples.)

Congratulations!

As with Volume 1, this is a great time to celebrate! In completing your inventory, examining your past has helped you understand how it has affected your present and your future. You most likely understand yourself like never before! Enjoy sharing the challenges with one another that you faced to complete this book and how you overcame those difficulties.

Your Next Step

Now you are ready to move to the next part of Principle 4: confessing your hurts, hang-ups, and habits to God, yourself, and another person you trust. Taking this step will move you into freedom from your past. Not only will you find freedom as you share the secrets of your past with another person, but you will also receive the "perfect freedom" of Christ's complete forgiveness for all your past shortcomings and sins. That's Good News!

Getting Right with God, Yourself, and Others

THE JOURNEY BEGINS

Introduction

Congratulations! You are well on your way on your road to recovery. You began by "Stepping Out of Denial into God's Grace." Next you made the major commitment to your continued growth in recovery by completing your spiritual inventory. That took a lot of effort and courage, but you will see some of the rewards of all your hard work as you finish Principle 4. The truth found in James 5:16 will take on new meaning in your life: "Confess your sins to each other and pray for each other so that you may be *healed*" (italics added).

After you CONFESS your sins, you will receive God's complete and perfect forgiveness. When you ADMIT your wrongs and share your inventory with another, you will experience further healing. As you become entirely READY to work through Principle 5, you will experience God's VICTORY in removing your defects of character that may have plagued you all your life.

Principle 6 will show you how to make your AMENDS and offer FORGIVENESS, so that you can be a model of God's GRACE as you get right with others.

In His steps,
John Baker

LESSON 12

Confess

Principle 4: Openly examine and confess my hurts, hang-ups, and habits to myself, to God, and to someone I trust.

Blessed are the pure in heart, for they will see God. (Matthew 5:8)

Step 5: We admitted to God, to ourselves, and to another human being the exact nature of our wrongs.

Therefore confess your sins to each other and pray for each other so that you may be healed. (James 5:16)

Think About It

After writing an inventory, we must deal with what we have written. The first way we do that is to confess our sins to God. Let's review the acrostic for CONFESS.

Confess your shortcomings, resentments, and sins

God wants us to come clean. He already knows all of our resentments, shortcomings and sins. Confession is just us telling Him we know them too.

Whoever conceals their sins does not prosper, but the one who confesses and renounces them finds mercy. (Proverbs 28:13)

Obey God's directions

Principle 4 sums up God's directions for confessing all of our resentments, shortcomings, and sins.

1. We confess to God.

It is written " 'As surely as I live,' says the Lord, 'every knee will bow before me; every tongue will acknowledge God.' " So then, each of us will give an account of ourselves to God. (Romans 14:11–12)

2. We share them with another person whom we trust:

Therefore confess your sins to each other and pray for each other so that you may be healed. The prayer of a righteous person is powerful and effective. (James 5:16)

No more guilt

This step begins to restore our confidence and our relationships and allows us to move on from our "rearview mirror" living. In Romans 8:1 we are assured that "there is now no condemnation for those who are in Christ Jesus."

CONFESS

For all have sinned and fall short of the glory of God, and all are justified freely by his grace through the redemption that came by Christ Jesus. (Romans 3:23–24)

The "CON" is over! We have followed God's directions on how to confess our wrongs. Four very positive things start to happen after we "FESS" up.

Face the truth

Recovery requires honesty! After we complete this principle we can allow the light of God's truth to heal our hurts, hang-ups, and habits. We stop denying our true feelings.

Create in me a pure heart, O God, and renew a steadfast spirit within me. Do not cast me from your presence or take your Holy Spirit from me. Restore to me the joy of your salvation and grant me a willing spirit, to sustain me. (Psalm 51:10–12)

Then you will know the truth, and the truth will set you free. (John 8:32)

Ease the pain

"We are only as sick as our secrets!" When we share our deepest secrets we divide the pain and the shame. We begin to see a healthy self-worth develop, one that is no longer based on the world's standards, but on those of Jesus Christ.

When I kept silent, my bones wasted away through my groaning all day long. For day and night your hand was heavy on me; my strength was sapped as in the heat of summer. Then I acknowledged my sin to you and did not cover up my iniquity. I said, "I will confess my transgressions to the LORD." And you forgave the guilt of my sin. (Psalm 32:3–5)

Stop the blame

We cannot find peace and serenity if we continue to blame ourselves or others. Our secrets have isolated us from each other. They have prevented intimacy in all our relationships.

"Why do you look at the speck of sawdust in your brother's eye and pay no attention to the plank in your own eye? How can you say to your brother, 'Let me take the speck out

of your eye,' when all the time there is a plank in your own eye? You hypocrite, first take the plank out of your own eye, and then you will see clearly to remove the speck from your brother's eye." (Matthew 7:3–5)

Start accepting God's forgiveness

Once we accept God's forgiveness we can look others in the eye. We understand ourselves and our past actions in a "new light." We are ready to find the humility to exchange our shortcomings in Principle 5.

Therefore, if anyone is in Christ, the new creation has come: The old has gone, the new is here! All this is from God, who reconciled us to himself through Christ and gave us the ministry of reconciliation: that God was reconciling the world to himself in Christ, not counting people's sins against them. And he has committed to us the message of reconciliation. (2 Corinthians 5:17–19)

If we confess our sins, he is faithful and just and will forgive us our sins and purify us from all unrighteousness. (1 John 1:9)

Write About It

1. What wrongs, resentments, or secret sins are keeping you awake at night? Wouldn't you like to get rid of them?

2. What value do you see in confessing, in coming clean of the wreckage of your past?

3. As you obey God's directions for confession, what results do you expect God to produce in your life?

4. What freedom do you feel because of the words of Romans 8:1 and Romans 3:23–24? What specifically do the phrases "no condemnation" and "not guilty" mean to you?

5. After you complete Principle 4, you will find four areas of your life begin to improve. You will be able to face the truth, ease the pain, stop the blame, and start accepting God's forgiveness. In what areas of your life will each of these four positive changes help your recovery?

   I can be more honest with . . .

   I can ease my pain by . . .

I can stop blaming . . .

I can accept God's forgiveness because of . . .

LESSON 13

Admit

Principle 4: Openly examine and confess my hurts, hang-ups, and habits to myself, to God, and to someone I trust.

Blessed are the pure in heart, for they will see God. (Matthew 5:8)

Step 5: We admitted to God, to ourselves, and to another human being the exact nature of our wrongs.

Therefore confess your sins to each other and pray for each other so that you may be healed. (James 5:16)

Think About It

People often ask me why they need to admit their wrongs to another person. There are three main reasons.

Why admit my hurts, hang-ups, and habits?

1. *We gain healing that the Bible promises.*

    Look at James 5:16 again. God's Word tells us that we are to admit our wrongs, our sins, to *one another*. You do this not to receive their forgiveness, for God already forgave you when you confessed your wrongs and sins to Him. James 5:16 says to confess your sins to one another for *healing*.

    Sharing our secret hurts, struggles, and failures with one another is part of God's plan of our healing process. The road to recovery is not meant to be walked alone.

2. *We gain freedom.*

    Our secrets have kept us in chains, bound up, frozen, and unable to move in all our relationships. Admitting our sins snaps the chains.

    Then they cried to the Lord in their trouble, and he saved them from their distress. He brought them out of darkness, the utter darkness, and broke away their chains." (Psalm 107:13–14)

3. *We gain support.*

    When you share your inventory with another person, you get support. Most important, the person will listen and not try to fix you!

How do I choose someone?
1. Choose someone of the same gender.
2. Ask your sponsor, accountability partner, or someone you trust. Just be sure they have completed Principle 4 (or Steps 4 and 5).
3. Set up an appointment with the person, a time without interruptions! It usually takes two to three hours to share your inventory.

ADMIT

Guidelines for your meeting

1. Start with prayer. Ask for courage, humility, and honesty. Here is a sample prayer:

   God, I ask that You fill me with Your peace and strength during my sharing of my inventory. Thank You for sending Your Son to pay the price for me, so my sins can be forgiven. During this meeting help me to be humble and completely honest. Help me to share all of the hurts from my past, so I can begin to find healing. Thank You for providing me with this program and _____ (the name of the person with whom you are sharing your inventory). Thank You for allowing the chains of my past to be snapped. In my Savior's name I pray, Amen.

2. Read the Principle 4 verses found on page 89 in this participant's guide.
3. Keep your sharing balanced—weaknesses and strengths!
4. End in prayer. Thank God for the tools He has given to you and for the complete forgiveness found in Christ!

If we confess our sins, he is faithful and just and will forgive us our sins and purify us from all unrighteousness. (1 John 1:9)

Write About It

1. In Principle 4 we are asked to give our inventory three times. Who are we to confess it to and why?

THE JOURNEY BEGINS

2. Most of us find it easier to confess our hurts and wrongs to ourselves and God. We seem to have more difficulty in sharing them with another person. What is the most difficult part for you? Why?

3. What is your biggest fear of sharing your inventory with another person?

4. List three people with whom you are considering sharing your inventory. List the pros and cons of each selection. Circle your final choice.

5. Pick a quiet location to share your inventory. List three places and circle the best one.

Now you are ready for one of the most freeing experiences of your life here on this earth! You will appreciate James 5:16 as never before: "Therefore confess your sins to each other and pray for each other so that you may be healed."

ADMIT

PRINCIPLE 4 VERSES

Therefore confess your sins to each other and pray for each other so that you may be healed. The prayer of a righteous person is powerful and effective. (James 5:16)

When you were dead in your sins and in the uncircumcision of your flesh, God made you alive with Christ. He forgave us all our sins, having canceled the charge of our legal indebtedness, which stood against us and condemned us; he has taken it away, nailing it to the cross. And having disarmed the powers and authorities, he made a public spectacle of them, triumphing over them by the cross. (Colossians 2:13–15)

If we claim to be without sin, we deceive ourselves and the truth is not in us. If we confess our sins, he is faithful and just and will forgive us our sins and purify us from all unrighteousness. (1 John 1:8–9)

Therefore, if anyone is in Christ, the new creation has come: The old has gone, the new is here! All this is from God, who reconciled us to himself through Christ and gave us the ministry of reconciliation: that God was reconciling the world to himself in Christ, not counting people's sins against them. And he has committed to us the message of reconciliation. (2 Corinthians 5:17–19)

Whoever conceals their sins does not prosper, but the one who confesses and renounces them finds mercy. (Proverbs 28:13)

It is written: " 'As surely as I live,' says the Lord, 'every knee will bow before me; every tongue will acknowledge God.' " So then, each of us will give an account of ourselves to God. (Romans 14:11–12)

Create in me a pure heart, O God, and renew a steadfast spirit within me. Do not cast me from your presence or take your Holy Spirit from me. Restore to me the joy of your salvation and grant me a willing spirit, to sustain me. (Psalm 51:10–12)

LESSON 14

Ready

Principle 5: Voluntarily submit to every change God wants to make in my life and humbly ask Him to remove my character defects.

Blessed are those who hunger and thirst for righteousness, for they will be filled. (Matthew 5:6)

Step 6: We were entirely ready to have God remove all these defects of character.

Humble yourselves before the Lord, and he will lift you up. (James 4:10)

Think About It

What does it mean to be entirely READY to have God remove our character defects?

Release control

In Principle 3, God didn't force His will on you. He waited for you to invite Him in! Now in Principle 5 you need to be entirely ready, willing to let God into every area of your life. He won't come in where He is not welcomed.

It has been said that "willingness is the key that goes into the lock and opens the door that allows God to begin to remove your character defects."

Teach me to do your will, for you are my God; may your good Spirit lead me on level ground. (Psalm 143:10)

Easy does it

These principles and steps are not quick fixes! You need to allow time for God to work in your life. *It takes time to find healing!*

The LORD is my strength and my shield; my heart trusts in him, and he helps me. My heart leaps for joy, and with my song I praise him. (Psalm 28:7)

Accept the change

Seeing the need for change and allowing the change to occur are two different things. Principle 5 will not work if you are still trapped by your self-will. You need to be ready to accept God's help throughout the transition.

Therefore, with minds that are alert and fully sober, set your hope on the grace to be brought to you when Jesus Christ is revealed at his coming. As obedient children, do not conform to the evil desires you had when you lived in ignorance. (1 Peter 1:13–14)

Do replace your character defects

You spent a lot of time with your old hurts, hang-ups, compulsions, obsessions, and habits. When God removes one, you need to replace it with something positive, such as time with God, recovery meetings, church and/or service! If you don't, you open yourself for a negative character defect to return.

"When an impure spirit comes out of a person, it goes through arid places seeking rest and does not find it. Then it says, 'I will return to the house I left.' When it arrives, it finds the house unoccupied, swept clean and put in order. Then it goes and takes with it seven other spirits more wicked than itself, and they go in and live there. And the final condition of that person is worse than the first. That is how it will be with this wicked generation." (Matthew 12:43–45)

Yield to the growth

Your old self-doubts and low self-esteem may tell you that you are not worthy of the growth and progress that you are making in the program. Yield to the growth—it is the Holy Spirit's work within you.

No one who is born of God will continue to sin, because God's seed remains in them; they cannot go on sinning, because they have been born of God. (1 John 3:9)

Are you entirely ready and willing to voluntarily submit to any and all changes God wants to make in your life? If you are, read the Principle 5a verses on pages 95 and 96 and pray the following prayer:

Dear God, thank You for taking me this far in my recovery journey. Now I pray for Your help in making me be entirely ready to change all my hang-ups and habits. Give me the strength to deal with all that I have turned over to You. Allow me to accept all the changes that You want to make in me. Help me be the person that You want me to be. In Your Son's name I pray, Amen.

Write About It

1. Have you released control? (If not, review Principle 3: "Consciously choose to commit all my life and will to Christ's care and control.")
   - List the areas of your life that you have been able to turn over and surrender to Jesus Christ.

   - List the areas of your life that you are still holding on to, attempting to control them on your own power.

2. What does the phrase "easy does it" mean to you? What area of your recovery are you attempting to rush—looking for the "quick fix"?

3. Explain the differences in seeing a need for change and being entirely ready to accept positive change in your recovery.

4. It is very important that you allow God to replace your character defects with positive changes. What are some of the positive changes that you could make in your recovery? In your family? In your job?

5. Sometimes it is difficult for us in recovery to see the positive changes that God is making in our lives. Have you been able to accept and enjoy your growth? How?

PRINCIPLE 5A VERSES

Humble yourselves before the Lord, and he will lift you up. (James 4:10)

Therefore, get rid of all moral filth and the evil that is so prevalent and humbly accept the word planted in you, which can save you. Do not merely listen to the word, and so deceive yourselves. Do what it says. (James 1:21–22)

I remember my affliction and my wandering, the bitterness and the gall. I well remember them, and my soul is downcast within me. Yet this I call to mind and therefore I have hope: Because of the LORD's great love we are not consumed, for his compassions never fail. (Lamentations 3:19–22)

Have mercy on me, O God, according to your unfailing love; according to your great compassion blot out my transgressions. Wash away all my iniquity and cleanse me from my sin. (Psalm 51:1–2)

THE JOURNEY BEGINS

Heal me, Lord, and I will be healed; save me and I will be saved, for you are the one I praise. (Jeremiah 17:14)

But he was pierced for our transgressions, he was crushed for our iniquities; the punishment that brought us peace was on him, and by his wounds we are healed. (Isaiah 53:5)

Then they cried to the Lord in their trouble, and he saved them from their distress. He sent out his word and healed them; he rescued them from the grave. Let them give thanks to the Lord for his unfailing love and his wonderful deeds for mankind. (Psalms 107:19–21)

Lord my God, I called to you for help, and you healed me. (Psalms 30:2)

LESSON 15

Victory

Principle 5: Voluntarily submit to every change God wants to make in my life and humbly ask Him to remove my character defects.

Blessed are those who hunger and thirst for righteousness, for they will be filled. (Matthew 5:6)

Step 6: We were entirely ready to have God remove all these defects of character.

Humble yourselves before the Lord, and he will lift you up. (James 4:10)

Step 7: We humbly asked Him to remove all our shortcomings.

If we confess our sins, he is faithful and just and will forgive us our sins and purify us from all unrighteousness. (1 John 1:9)

Think About It

How can you have VICTORY over your defects of character?

Voluntarily submit

Voluntarily submit to every change God wants me to make in my life and humbly ask Him to remove my shortcomings.

Therefore, I urge you, brothers and sisters, in view of God's mercy, to offer your bodies as a living sacrifice, holy and pleasing to God—this is your true and proper worship. Do not conform to the pattern of this world, but be transformed by the renewing of your mind. Then you will be able to test and approve what God's will is—his good, pleasing and perfect will. (Romans 12:1–2)

In Principle 3 we made a decision to turn our lives over to God's will. Now you are "entirely ready to have God remove all [your] defects of character" (Step 6).

It is important to understand that Principle 5 is a process. Lasting change takes time. The remainder of this lesson outlines the process to have God make the positive changes in your life that you and He both desire.

Identify character defects

Identify which character defects you want to work on first. Go back to the wrongs, shortcomings, and compulsive behaviors you discovered in your inventory. Ask God to first remove those that are causing the most pain.

In their hearts humans plan their course, but the LORD establishes their steps. (Proverbs 16:9)

Change your mind

When you become a Christian you are a new creation—a brand new person inside; the old nature is gone. But you have to let God transform (change) you by renewing your mind. The changes that are going to take place are a result of a team effort—your responsibility is to take the action to follow God's directions for change.

Do not conform to the pattern of this world, but be transformed by the renewing of your mind. Then you will be able to test and approve what God's will is—his good, pleasing and perfect will. (Romans 12:2)

Turn over character defects

Turn your character defects over to Jesus Christ. Relying on your own willpower has blocked your recovery. You have tried to change your hurts, hang-ups, and habits by yourself and were unsuccessful. "Let go; let God."

Humble yourselves before the Lord, and he will lift you up. (James 4:10)

The Lord is faithful, and he will strengthen you and protect you from the evil one. (2 Thessalonians 3:3)

One day at a time

Recovery works one day at a time! Your lifelong hurts, hang-ups, and habits need to be worked on in twenty-four-hour increments. "Life by the yard is hard; life by the inch is a cinch."

Therefore do not worry about tomorrow, for tomorrow will worry about itself. Each day has enough trouble of its own. (Matthew 6:34)

Recovery is a process

Once you ask God to remove your character defects, you begin a journey that will lead you to new freedom from your past. Don't look for perfection; instead rejoice in steady progress.

In all my prayers for all of you, I always pray with joy because of your partnership in the gospel from the first day until now, being confident of this, that he who began a good work in you will carry it on to completion until the day of Christ Jesus. (Philippians 1:4–6)

You must choose to change

To ask for help to change your hurts, hang-ups, and habits requires humility. We need to stop trying to make the changes on our power. We need to "humbly ask Him to remove all our shortcomings." We need to rely on His power to change us!

THE JOURNEY BEGINS

But he gives us more grace. That is why Scripture says: "God opposes the proud but shows favor to the humble." Submit yourselves, then, to God. Resist the devil, and he will flee from you. Come near to God and he will come near to you. Wash your hands, you sinners, and purify your hearts, you double-minded. (James 4:6–8)

PRINCIPLE 5 PRAYER

Dear God, show me Your will in working on my shortcomings. Help me not to resist the changes that You have planned for me. I need You to "direct my steps." Help me stay in today, not get dragged back into the past or lost in the future. I ask You to give me the power and the wisdom to make the very best I can out of today. In Christ's name I pray, Amen.

Write About It

1. As you *voluntarily* submit to every change God wants you to make in your recovery, how does Romans 12:1–2 help you know that real, positive change is possible?

2. In Principle 5 you need to ask God to help you identify the defects of character that you need to work on first. List the changes that you want to ask God to help you work on now. Will you work on them?

3. God's Word teaches us that real change comes from the changing of our minds. We must take the positive action required to follow God's directions. List the actions that you need to take to begin working on the defects of character that you listed in question 2.
    ACTION PLAN
    (Read the Principle 5b verses on page 102.)

Defect of character:

I need to stop doing:

I need to start doing:

4. List the specific ways that you have turned from relying on your own willpower to relying on God's will for your life.

5. What does the phrase "one day at a time" mean to you and your recovery?

6. It has been stated that "Recovery is not perfection; it is a process." Do you agree with that? Why?

7. What does humility mean to you? How will being humble allow you to change?

PRINCIPLE 5B VERSES

If we confess our sins, he is faithful and just and will forgive us our sins and purify us from all unrighteousness. (1 John 1:9)

Therefore, I urge you, brothers and sisters, in view of God's mercy, to offer your bodies as a living sacrifice, holy and pleasing to God—this is your true and proper worship. Do not conform to the pattern of this world, but be transformed by the renewing of your mind. Then you will be able to test and approve what God's will is—his good, pleasing and perfect will. (Romans 12:1–2)

If any of you lacks wisdom, you should ask God, who gives generously to all without finding fault, and it will be given to you. But when you ask, you must believe and not doubt, because the one who doubts is like a wave of the sea, blown and tossed by the wind. (James 1:5–6)

But he gives us more grace. That is why Scripture says: "God opposes the proud but shows favor to the humble." Submit yourselves, then, to God. Resist the devil, and he will flee from you. Come near to God and he will come near to you. Wash your hands, you sinners, and purify your hearts, you double-minded. Grieve, mourn and wail. Change your laughter to mourning and your joy to gloom. Humble yourselves before the Lord, and he will lift you up. (James 4:6–10)

Now to him who is able to do immeasurably more than all we ask or imagine, according to his power that is at work within us, to him be glory in the church and in Christ Jesus throughout all generations, for ever and ever! Amen. (Ephesians 3:20–21)

LESSON 16

Amends

Principle 6: Evaluate all my relationships. Offer forgiveness to those who have hurt me and make amends for harm I've done to others, except when to do so would harm them or others.

Blessed are the merciful, for they will be shown mercy. (Matthew 5:7)

Blessed are the peacemakers, for they will be called children of God. (Matthew 5:9)

Step 8: We made a list of all persons we had harmed and became willing to make amends to them all.

Do to others as you would have them do to you. (Luke 6:31)

Think About It

Making your amends is the beginning of the end of your isolation from others and God. The AMENDS acrostic will help you get started.

<u>A</u>dmit the hurt and the harm

In this step/principle, you will work on forgiving those who have hurt you, and offering your amends to the people you have hurt. You need to once again face the hurts, resentments, and wrongs others have caused you, or wrongs that you have caused others. Holding on to resentments blocks your recovery.

"Do not judge, and you will not be judged. Do not condemn, and you will not be condemned. Forgive, and you will be forgiven." (Luke 6:37)

Bear with each other and forgive one another if any of you has a grievance against someone. Forgive as the Lord forgave you. (Colossians 3:13)

<u>M</u>ake a list

Go back to your inventory sheets. In column 1 you will find the list of people who you need to forgive. In column 5 you will find the list of people to whom you owe amends. Are there any others you need to add?

Do to others as you would have them do to you. (Luke 6:31)

Be kind and compassionate to one another, forgiving each other, just as in Christ God forgave you. (Ephesians 4:32)

<u>E</u>ncourage one another

Before you make your amends to others you need to meet with your accountability partner or a sponsor. They will encourage you and give you a valuable objective opinion, which will ensure that your motives stay on track.

And let us consider how we may spur one another on toward love and good deeds. (Hebrews 10:24)

Not for them

You need to approach those to whom you are offering your amends humbly, sincerely, and willingly. Do not offer excuses or attempt to justify your actions. Focus only on your part. Don't expect anything back.

But love your enemies, do good to them, and lend to them without expecting to get anything back. Then your reward will be great, and you will be children of the Most High, because he is kind to the ungrateful and wicked. Be merciful, just as your Father is merciful. (Luke 6:35–36)

Do it at the right time

This step not only requires courage, good judgment, and willingness, but a careful sense of timing! It is *key* at this time to prayerfully ask Jesus Christ for His guidance and direction.

Wait for the LORD; be strong and take heart and wait for the LORD. (Psalms 27:14)

Let us not become weary in doing good, for at the proper time we will reap a harvest if we do not give up. Therefore, as we have opportunity, let us do good to all people, especially to those who belong to the family of believers. (Galatians 6:9–10)

Start living the promises of recovery

As we complete this principle, we will discover God's gift of true freedom from our past. We will begin to find the peace and serenity that we have long been seeking. We will become ready to embrace God's purpose for our lives.

God promises, "I will repay you for the years the locusts have eaten" (Joel 2:25).

If it is possible, as far as it depends on you, live at peace with everyone. (Romans 12:18)

THE JOURNEY BEGINS
PRINCIPLE 6A PRAYER

Dear God, I pray for willingness—willingness to evaluate all my past and current relationships. Please show me the people who I have hurt, and help me become willing to offer my amends to them. Also, God, give me Your strength to become willing to forgive those who have hurt me. I pray for Your perfect timing for taking the action Principle 6 calls for. I ask all these things in Your Son's name, Amen.

Write About It

1. Explain how holding on to your past resentments and guilt has blocked your recovery. Be specific.

2. Next, you are ready to make your list. Use the following worksheet. List the names of those to whom you think you owe an amends. Keep this chart and see how God has increased your list within the next thirty days. Also, begin praying for the willingness and God's direction for you to complete this principle.

Amends List

    I owe amends to . . .

    I need to forgive...

AMENDS

3. Who do you have on your recovery support team to encourage you as you make your amends?

   SPONSOR:

   ACCOUNTABILITY PARTNERS:

4. What does the phrase "not for them" mean to you?

5. What does the phrase "don't expect anything back" mean to you?

6. Timing is so important in this step. List the individuals who could be possibly injured from your making an amends to them and why.

7. Go back to the "start living the promises" section of amends. List some of the promises of recovery that are coming true in your life!

LESSON 17

Forgiveness

Principle 6: Evaluate all my relationships. Offer forgiveness to those who have hurt me and make amends for harm I've done to others, except when to do so would harm them or others.

Blessed are the merciful, for they will be shown mercy. (Matthew 5:7)

Blessed are the peacemakers, for they will be called children of God. (Matthew 5:9)

Step 8: We made a list of all persons we had harmed and became willing to make amends to them all.

Do to others as you would have them do to you. (Luke 6:31)

Step 9: We made direct amends to such people whenever possible, except when to do so would injure them or others.

"Therefore, if you are offering your gift at the altar and there remember that your brother or sister has something against you, leave your gift there in front of the altar. First go and be reconciled to them; then come and offer your gift." (Matthew 5:23–24)

Think About It

Do you know the three kinds of forgiveness? To be completely free from your resentments, anger, fears, shame, and guilt, you need to give and accept forgiveness in all areas of your life. If you do not, your recovery will be stalled and thus incomplete.

Have you accepted God's forgiveness?

Have you really accepted Jesus' work on the cross? By His death on the cross all your sins were canceled—*paid in full!* He exclaimed from the cross, "'It is finished'" (John 19:30).

This righteousness is given through faith in Jesus Christ to all who believe. There is no difference between Jew and Gentile, for all have sinned and fall short of the glory of God, and all are justified freely by his grace through the redemption that came by Christ Jesus. God presented Christ as a sacrifice of atonement, through the shedding of his blood—to be received by faith. He did this to demonstrate his righteousness, because in his forbearance he had left the sins committed beforehand unpunished—he did it to demonstrate his righteousness at the present time, so as to be just and the one who justifies those who have faith in Jesus. (Romans 3:22–26)

Have you forgiven others who have hurt you?

You must "let go" of the pain of the past caused by others. Until you are able to release it and forgive it, it will continue to hold you prisoner.

Do not repay anyone evil for evil. Be careful to do what is right in the eyes of everyone. If it is possible, as far as it depends on you, live at peace with everyone. (Romans 12:17–18)

Be kind and compassionate to one another, forgiving each other, just as in Christ God forgave you. (Ephesians 4:32)

Offering forgiveness to others can look one of three ways:

1. Forgiving others in our hearts and minds. This is a forgiveness that takes place in our hearts, when verbally communicating our forgiveness is not safe or possible.
2. Verbally offering our forgiveness to others. Pray and ask God to guide you to which is best for your situation.
3. Writing a letter to someone who is unsafe (you may choose to send letter or not send the letter) or to someone who may have passed away.

Pray and ask God to guide you to which is best for your situation.

NOTE: If you have been the victim of sexual abuse, physical abuse, or childhood emotional abuse or neglect I am truly sorry for the pain you have suffered. I hurt with you. But you will not find the peace and freedom from your perpetrator until you are able to forgive that person. Remember, forgiving him or her in no way excuses the harm done against you. Forgiveness will allow you, however, to be released from the power that the person has had over you. I have rewritten Steps 8 and 9 for you.

Step 8: Make a list of all persons who have harmed us and become willing to seek God's help in forgiving our perpetrators, as well as forgiving ourselves. Realize we've also harmed others and become willing to make amends to them.

Step 9: Extend forgiveness to ourselves and to others who have perpetrated against us, realizing this is an attitude of the heart, not always confrontation. Make direct amends, asking forgiveness from those people we have harmed, except when to do so would injure them or others.

<u>Have you forgiven yourself?</u>

You may feel that the guilt and shame of your past is just too much to forgive. This is what God wants you to do with the darkness of your past: "'Come now, let us settle the matter,' says the Lord. 'Though your sins are like scarlet, they shall be as white as snow; though they are red as crimson, they shall be like wool'" (Isaiah 1:18).

Remember Romans 8:1, "Therefore, there is now no condemnation for those who are in Christ Jesus."

Write About It

1. As you look at the three kinds of forgiveness, which one of them was the easiest for you to accept? Why?

2. Which area of forgiveness was the most difficult for you to accept? Why?

3. What do the words of Christ found in John 19:30 ("'It is finished.'") mean to you?

4. What hurt(s) from a past relationship are you still holding on to?

5. How can you let go of the hurt(s)? Be specific.

6. How have you been blaming God for the harmful actions that others took against you?

7. Have you forgiven yourself? What past actions in your life do you still feel guilt and shame about? (List them, pray about them, and work on them in the next lesson.)

8. Make a "Forgiveness List" of those who have hurt you. (This is column 1 from your inventory.) Pray that God helps you to become willing to forgive them, and reveals whether this should be verbally communicated (or in the form of a letter you may or may not mail), or an attitude of the heart.

PRINCIPLE 6A VERSES

Do to others as you would have them do to you. (Luke 6:31)

Bear with each other and forgive one another if any of you has a grievance against someone. Forgive as the Lord forgave you. (Colossians 3:13)

Be kind and compassionate to one another, forgiving each other, just as in Christ God forgave you. (Ephesians 4:32)

"Do not judge, and you will not be judged. Do not condemn, and you will not be condemned. Forgive, and you will be forgiven." (Luke 6:37)

And forgive us our debts, as we also have forgiven our debtors. (Matthew 6:12)

What, then, shall we say in response to these things? If God is for us, who can be against us? (Romans 8:31)

THE JOURNEY BEGINS

Let us not become weary in doing good, for at the proper time we will reap a harvest if we do not give up. Therefore, as we have opportunity, let us do good to all people, especially to those who belong to the family of believers. (Galatians 6:9–10)

"Therefore, if you are offering your gift at the altar and there remember that your brother or sister has something against you, leave your gift there in front of the altar. First go and be reconciled to them; then come and offer your gift." (Matthew 5:23–24)

LESSON 18

Grace

Principle 6: Evaluate all my relationships. Offer forgiveness to those who have hurt me and make amends for harm I've done to others, except when to do so would harm them or others.

Blessed are the merciful, for they will be shown mercy. (Matthew 5:7)

Blessed are the peacemakers, for they will be called children of God. (Matthew 5:9)

Step 9: We made direct amends to such people whenever possible, except when to do so would injure them or others.

"Therefore, if you are offering your gift at the altar and there remember that your brother or sister has something against you, leave your gift there in front of the altar. First go and be reconciled to them; then come and offer your gift." (Matthew 5:23–24)

Think About It

To complete Principle 6 we make our amends, make restitution, offer our forgiveness, but most of all, we must receive and model Jesus Christ's freely given gift of GRACE.

But he said to me, "My grace is sufficient for you, for my power is made perfect in weakness." Therefore I will boast all the more gladly about my weaknesses, so that Christ's power may rest on me. That is why, for Christ's sake, I delight in weaknesses, in insults, in hardships, in persecutions, in difficulties. For when I am weak, then I am strong. (2 Corinthians 12:9–10)

God's gift

Grace cannot be bought. It is a freely given gift by God to you and me. When we complete Principle 6, we are to offer (give) our amends and forgiveness and expect nothing back.

For all have sinned and fall short of the glory of God, and all are justified freely by his grace through the redemption that came by Christ Jesus. (Romans 3:23–24)

Therefore, with minds that are alert and fully sober, set your hope on the grace to be brought to you when Jesus Christ is revealed at his coming. (1 Peter 1:13)

Received by our faith

We cannot work our way into heaven. Only by professing our faith in Christ as our Savior can we experience His grace and have eternal life. It is only through our faith in Christ that we can find the strength and courage needed for us to make our amends and offer our forgiveness.

For it is by grace you have been saved, through faith—and this is not from yourselves, it is the gift of God—not by works, so that no one can boast. (Ephesians 2:8–9)

Therefore, since we have been justified through faith, we have peace with God through our Lord Jesus Christ, through whom we have gained access by faith into this grace in which we now stand. And we boast in the hope of the glory of God. (Romans 5:1–2)

Accepted by God's love

God loved us while we were still sinning. Grace is the love that gives, that loves the unlovely and the unlovable. We can love others because God first loved us, and we can also forgive others because God first forgave us.

But God demonstrates his own love for us in this: While we were still sinners, Christ died for us. (Romans 5:8)

Forgive us our debts, as we also have forgiven our debtors. (Matthew 6:12)

Let us then approach God's throne of grace with confidence, so that we may receive mercy and find grace to help us in our time of need. (Hebrews 4:16)

Christ paid the price

Jesus loves us so much that He died on the cross so that all our sins, all our wrongs, are forgiven. He paid the price and sacrificed Himself for us so that we may be with Him forever. We also need to sacrifice—our pride and our selfishness. We must speak the truth in love and focus on our part in making amends or offering forgiveness.

"I do not set aside the grace of God, for if righteousness could be gained through the law, Christ died for nothing!" (Galatians 2:21)

In him we have redemption through his blood, the forgiveness of sins, in accordance with the riches of God's grace. (Ephesians 1:7)

Everlasting gift

Once you have accepted Jesus Christ as your Lord and Savior, God's gift of grace is forever.

For I am convinced that neither death nor life, neither angels nor demons, neither the present nor the future, nor any powers, neither height nor depth, nor anything else in all creation, will be able to separate us from the love of God that is in Christ Jesus our Lord. (Romans 8:38–39)

THE JOURNEY BEGINS

May our Lord Jesus Christ himself and God our Father, who loved us and by his grace gave us eternal encouragement and good hope, encourage your hearts and strengthen you in every good deed and word. (2 Thessalonians 2:16–17)

Now you are ready to start modeling God's grace by working Principle 6.

1. Take the names of the individuals that you listed on your "Amends List" (page 106) and "Forgiveness List" (page 113).
2. Highlight the ones you can take care of immediately.
3. Review them one more time with your sponsor or accountability partner to ensure that making an amends or offering your forgiveness to the individual would not injure them or another.
4. Pray, asking God to show you the right time to make the amends or offer your forgiveness. Read the Principle 6b verses on page 121.
5. Develop a plan for making amends to those on your list that you cannot make immediately. If someone on your list has died or you cannot locate him or her, you can write the person a letter and share it with your support team.

PRINCIPLE 6B PRAYER

Dear God, thank You for Your love, for Your freely given grace. Help me model Your ways when I make my amends to those I have hurt and offer my forgiveness to those who have injured me. Help me to set aside my selfishness and speak the truth in love. I pray that I would focus only on my part, my responsibility in the issue. I know that I can forgive others because You first forgave me. Thank You for loving me. In Jesus' name I pray, Amen.

Write About It

1. How has Jesus Christ used your weaknesses and turned them into strengths?

2. How can you receive God's gift of grace (Romans 5:2)?

3. How can you model God's gift of grace in making your amends?

4. In what ways have you experienced God's grace in your recovery?

5. God loved and accepted us while we were still sinners (Ephesians 2:5). How can you model that acceptance to those to whom you need to offer forgiveness or make amends?

6. In Principle 6 we are not trying to get even. Christ paid the price for all of our wrongs. What does "speaking the truth in love" mean to you?

7. Why is it important that you focus only on your part in making an amends or offering forgiveness?

8. List some of the things that God has shown you through working Principle 6.

GRACE

PRINCIPLE 6B VERSES

But because of his great love for us, God, who is rich in mercy, made us alive with Christ even when we were dead in transgressions—it is by grace you have been saved. (Ephesians 2:4–5)

Whoever claims to love God yet hates a brother or sister is a liar. For whoever does not love their brother and sister, whom they have seen, cannot love God, whom they have not seen. (1 John 4:20)

But love your enemies, do good to them, and lend to them without expecting to get anything back. Then your reward will be great, and you will be children of the Most High, because he is kind to the ungrateful and wicked. (Luke 6:35)

"You have heard that it was said, 'Love your neighbor and hate your enemy.' But I tell you, love your enemies and pray for those who persecute you, that you may be children of your Father in heaven. He causes his sun to rise on the evil and the good, and sends rain on the righteous and the unrighteous." (Matthew 5:43–45)

Do not repay anyone evil for evil. Be careful to do what is right in the eyes of everyone. If it is possible, as far as it depends on you, live at peace with everyone. (Romans 12:17–18)

Let no debt remain outstanding, except the continuing debt to love one another, for whoever loves others has fulfilled the law. (Romans 13:8)

Congratulations!

It's time to celebrate again! Undoubtedly, your relationships to many in your group are closer than ever. Putting aside a time to share about completing another step forward in your recovery, helps to internalize the name of the program, "Celebrate Recovery". You can also celebrate that you are approaching the last stage of your step study group!

Your Next Step

The freedom you found by working Principles 4 through 6 can only come from God and a lot of courageous effort from you. You have taken a giant step toward "getting right with God, yourself, and others!"

Remember that recovery is a journey, a process. God and you are going to be working on the changes in your life for many years to come, one day at a time!

Now you are ready for the last two principles of the program. Principles 7 and 8 are going to show you how to continue "Growing in Christ While Helping Others."

VOLUME 4

Growing in Christ While Helping Others

THE JOURNEY BEGINS

Introduction

Congratulations! You have made it through the first six principles on your road to recovery. You began your journey by "Stepping Out of Denial into God's Grace." Then you faced the good and bad of your past by "Taking an Honest and Spiritual Inventory." And you just spent the last several months "Getting Right with God, Yourself, and Others."

Now you are ready to begin working on the last two principles along the road to recovery. These principles are much more than maintenance. As you practice them, they will help you continue "Growing in Christ While Helping Others," one day at a time!

Principle 7 is when you learn to take a daily INVENTORY and stand at the CROSSROADS of your recovery. You begin to live in newfound freedom in Christ. You learn that the best way to prevent a RELAPSE is to continue to grow in Christ through your quiet time and Bible study. In addition, Principle 7 will help you keep an "attitude of GRATITUDE."

And finally, in Principle 8 you will understand how important it is to GIVE back to others what you have learned in your journey. Jesus will give you the courage to step out and say "YES" to helping newcomers and serving others.

In working with others, as sponsors or accountability partners, it is important for you to know the areas and reasons that can cause them to get stuck along their road to recovery. Lesson 25 includes the SEVEN REASONS WE GET STUCK IN OUR RECOVERIES.

After each lesson, there is an exercise for you to complete. Answer each question to the best of your ability. Don't worry about what you think the answer *should* be. Pray and then write down the answer from your heart. Remember John 8:32: "Then you will know the truth, and the truth will set you free."

After you have completed the exercise, share it with someone you trust. Your group, an accountability partner, or your sponsor (these are explained in Volume 2, Lesson 7) are all safe choices. You do not recover from your hurts, hang-ups, and habits by just attending recovery meetings. You must work and live the principles!

Now get ready for the rest of the journey that God has planned for you as you celebrate your recovery—one day at a time!

In His steps,
John Baker

LESSON 19

Crossroads

Principle 7: Reserve a daily time with God for self-examination, Bible reading, and prayer in order to know God and His will for my life and to gain the power to follow His will.

Step 10: We continued to take personal inventory, and when we were wrong, promptly admitted it.

So, if you think you are standing firm, be careful that you don't fall!
(1 Corinthians 10:12)

THE JOURNEY BEGINS

Think About It

"Jesus said, 'If you hold to my teaching, you are really my disciples. Then you will know the truth, and the truth will set you free'" (John 8:31–32). By working the principles and following Christ's directions, the foundation of your life has been rebuilt. You will undoubtedly see major changes in your life, if you haven't already! But now you are at the CROSSROADS of your recovery.

First Corinthians 10:12 warns us, "So, if you think you are standing firm, be careful that you don't fall!" Steps 10 through 12 (Principles 7 and 8) are where we will live out our recoveries for the rest of our time here on earth. They are much more than maintenance steps, as some have referred to them. These are the "how I want to live the rest of my life" steps and principles.

As we begin to work Step 10[1], we will see that it is made up of three key parts, each one corresponding to the acrostic for this lesson, TEN.

Take time to do a daily inventory

1. The *what*: "We continued to take personal inventory . . ."

Let us examine our ways and test them, and let us return to the LORD. *(Lamentations 3:40)*

Evaluate the good and the bad parts of our day

2. The *why*: ". . . and when we were wrong . . ."

If we claim to be without sin, we deceive ourselves and the truth is not in us. If we confess our sins, he is faithful and just and will forgive us our sins and purify us from all unrighteousness. If we claim we have not sinned, we make him out to be a liar and his word is not in us. (1 John 1:8–10)

---

1. Please note that though Step 10 and Principle 7 differ somewhat in their focus, both point toward the same result: the character and image of Christ in our daily life. This chapter will emphasize the step more than the principle, but in no way do we intend to discount the many benefits of daily living in Principle 7.

Need to admit our wrongs promptly

3. The *then what*: "... promptly admitted it."

"Therefore, if you are offering your gift at the altar and there remember that your brother or sister has something against you, leave your gift there in front of the altar. First go and be reconciled to them; then come and offer your gift." (Matthew 5:23–24)

Practice keeping a daily journal for one week. Write out your daily inventory—the good and the bad. Look for negative patterns, issues that you are repeatedly writing down and having to promptly make amends for! Share them with your sponsor or accountability partner, and set up an action plan for you—with God's help and power—to overcome them.

Write About It

1. Before you start working on Step 10, take a moment to reflect and list some of the changes in your life that have come from working the steps and principles with Jesus as your Higher Power.
   - How has your behavior changed?

   - What specific relationships have been restored or improved?

   - How has your relationship with Jesus grown since you began your journey of recovery?

- List the new relationships that you have made along your journey.

2. In your own words, what does Step 10 mean to you?
   - The *what*: "We continued to take personal inventory . . ."

   - The *why*: ". . . and when we were wrong . . ."

   - The *then what*: ". . . promptly admitted it."

3. Keep a daily journal over the next seven days. Record the good along with the bad. Write down victories and areas of needed growth. Look for patterns. Share them with your sponsor or accountability partner at the end of the week.

Your Step 10 Journal
Day One

Day Two

Day Three

Day Four

Day Five

THE JOURNEY BEGINS

Day Six

Day Seven

4. What did you learn by keeping your journal?

5. What areas did you identify as strengths?

6. What areas do you need to work on?

Suggestion: It's a Healthy Habit!

Keeping a daily journal is a key tool to help you stay on track on your road to recovery. You've done it for seven days, why stop now?

LESSON
20

Daily Inventory

Principle 7: Reserve a daily time with God for self-examination, Bible reading, and prayer in order to know God and His will for my life and to gain the power to follow His will.

Step 10: We continued to take personal inventory and when we were wrong, promptly admitted it.

So, if you think you are standing firm, be careful that you don't fall!
(1 Corinthians 10:12)

Think About It

In Principle 7 and Step 10, we begin to apply what we have discovered in the first six principles and nine steps: We humbly live in reality, not denial; we have done our best to make amends for our past; we desire to grow daily in our new relationships with Jesus Christ and others.

God has provided us with a daily checklist for our new lifestyle. It's called the "Great Commandment":

Jesus replied: " 'Love the Lord your God with all your heart and with all your soul and with all your mind.' This is the first and greatest commandment. And the second is like it: 'Love your neighbor as yourself.' All the Law and the Prophets hang on these two commandments." (Matthew 22:37–40)

James 1:22 encourages us: "Do not merely listen to the word, and so deceive yourselves. Do what it says." When we practice the Great Commandment, we become doers of God's Word, living examples of Christ. Our walk lines up with our talk! The apostle Paul lived that way. He says in 1 Thessalonians 1:4–5, "For we know, brothers and sisters loved by God, that he has chosen you, because our gospel came to you not simply with words but also with power, with the Holy Spirit and deep conviction. You know how we lived among you for your sake."

There are three ways to do a Step 10 inventory.

Ongoing

We can do this periodically throughout the day. The best time to admit we are wrong is the exact time that we are made aware of it! Why wait? We need to make amends ASAP! We will sleep a lot better at night!

Daily

At the end of each day we need to look over our daily activities—the good and the bad. We need to search for where we might have harmed someone or where we acted out of anger or fear. The best way to do this is to keep a journal! Then the next morning as promptly as we can, we need to admit mistakes and make our amends.

DAILY INVENTORY

Periodic

Every three months, get away for a "mini retreat." Bring your daily journal with you. Pray and read your daily entries. Ask God to show you areas in your life that you can improve over the next ninety days and the victories that you have made in the last ninety days!

The Bible gives us instructions on how to avoid the necessity of making an amends in Step 10:

Whoever conceals hatred with lying lips and spreads slander is a fool. Sin is not ended by multiplying words, but the prudent hold their tongues. (Proverbs 10:18–19)

Do not let any unwholesome talk come out of your mouths, but only what is helpful for building others up according to their needs, that it may benefit those who listen. (Ephesians 4:29)

The wise in heart are called discerning, and gracious words promote instruction. Prudence is a fountain of life to the prudent, but folly brings punishment to fools. The hearts of the wise make their mouths prudent, and their lips promote instruction. (Proverbs 16:21–23)

Anxiety weighs down the heart, but a kind word cheers it up. (Proverbs 12:25)

If I speak in the tongues of men or of angels, but do not have love, I am only a resounding gong or a clanging cymbal. (1 Corinthians 13:1)

Step 10 daily action plan

1. Continue to take a daily inventory, and when you are wrong, promptly make your amends.
2. Summarize the events of your day in your journal.
3. Read and memorize one of the Step 10 verses (see above).
4. Work all steps and principles to the best of your ability.

The key verse for this lesson is Mark 14:38: "Watch and pray so that you will not fall into temptation. The spirit is willing, but the flesh is weak."

THE JOURNEY BEGINS

PRINCIPLE 7A PRAYER

Dear God, thank You for today. Thank You for giving me the tools to work my program and live my life differently, centered in Your will. Lord, help me to make my amends promptly and ask for forgiveness. In all my relationships today help me to do my part in making them healthy and growing. In Jesus' name I pray, Amen.

Write About It

1. What are some of the advantages of each of the three types of inventories in your recovery? How can they help you to "be careful that you don't fall"?
   - Ongoing:

   - Daily:

   - Periodic (monthly, quarterly, or annually):

2. What do the following verses mean to you and how can they help you in this step?

Whoever conceals hatred with lying lips and spreads slander is a fool. Sin is not ended by multiplying words, but the prudent hold their tongues. (Proverbs 10:18–19)

DAILY INVENTORY

Do not let any unwholesome talk come out of your mouths, but only what is helpful for building others up according to their needs, that it may benefit those who listen. (Ephesians 4:29)

The wise in heart are called discerning, and gracious words promote instruction. Prudence is a fountain of life to the prudent, but folly brings punishment to fools. The hearts of the wise make their mouths prudent, and their lips promote instruction. (Proverbs 16:21–23)

Anxiety weighs down the heart, but a kind word cheers it up. (Proverbs 12:25)

If I speak in the tongues of men or of angels, but do not have love, I am only a resounding gong or a clanging cymbal. (1 Corinthians 13:1)

Watch and pray so that you will not fall into temptation. The spirit is willing, but the flesh is weak. (Mark 14:38)

3. What is your daily action plan for Step 10?

4. What are the recurring events or issues that you are constantly needing to make amends for?
   - With your family?

   - With your friends?

   - With those you work with?

   - With those in your church or recovery program?

DAILY INVENTORY

PRINCIPLE 7A VERSES

For by the grace given me I say to every one of you: Do not think of yourself more highly than you ought, but rather think of yourself with sober judgment, in accordance with the faith God has distributed to each of you. (Romans 12:3)

Because you are my help I sing in the shadow of your wings. I cling to you; your right hand upholds me. (Psalm 63:7–8)

Test me, Lord, and try me, examine my heart and my mind; for I have always been mindful of your unfailing love and have lived in reliance on your faithfulness. (Psalm 26:2–3)

A person may think their own ways are right, but the Lord weighs the heart. (Proverbs 21:2)

The prudent see danger and take refuge, but the simple keep going and pay the penalty. (Proverbs 27:12)

Watch your life and doctrine closely. Persevere in them, because if you do, you will save both yourself and your hearers. (1 Timothy 4:16)

So, if you think you are standing firm, be careful that you don't fall! (1 Corinthians 10:12)

Consider it pure joy, my brothers and sisters, whenever you face trials of many kinds, because you know that the testing of your faith produces perseverance. (James 1:2–3)

A heart at peace gives life to the body, but envy rots the bones. (Proverbs 14:30)

LESSON 21

Relapse

Principle 7: Reserve a daily time with God for self-examination, Bible reading, and prayer in order to know God and His will for my life and to gain the power to follow His will.

Step 11: We sought through prayer and meditation to improve our conscious contact with God, praying only for knowledge of His will for us and power to carry that out.

Let the message of Christ dwell among you richly. (Colossians 3:16)

Think About It

The best ways to prevent relapse can be summarized in the acrostic RELAPSE. Although relapse can be easy to define in some recovery issues, it may be hard to define in others. For those where sobriety is hard to define or not applicable, part of your recovery process is defining what relapse would look like for your recovery issue. Talking with your support team can help with this.

Reserve a daily quiet time

Principle 7 sums it up best: Reserve a daily time with God for self-examination, Bible reading, and prayer in order to know God and His will for my life and gain the power to follow His will.

"Watch and pray so that you will not fall into temptation. The spirit is willing, but the flesh is weak." (Mark 14:38)

Evaluate

Your evaluation needs to include your physical, emotional, relational, and spiritual health. And don't forget the value of doing a "H-E-A-R-T" check. Are you. . .

Hurting
Exhausted
Angry
Resentful
Tense?

Special instructions for this step are found in Psalm 16:7–10: "I will praise the Lord, who counsels me; even at night my heart instructs me. I keep my eyes always on the Lord. With him at my right hand, I will not be shaken. Therefore my heart is glad and my tongue rejoices; my body also will rest secure, because you will not abandon me to the realm of the dead, nor will you let your faithful one see decay."

Listen to Jesus

We need to take a time-out from the world's "rat race" long enough to listen to our bodies, our minds, and our souls. We need to slow down enough to hear the Lord's directions.

The LORD is my shepherd, I lack nothing. He makes me lie down in green pastures, he leads me beside quiet waters, he refreshes my soul. He guides me along the right paths for his name's sake. (Psalm 23:1–3)

Your word is a lamp for my feet, a light on my path. (Psalm 119:105)

Alone and quiet time

Jesus Christ spent time alone with His Father. You need to do the same. Set a daily appointment time to be alone with God. Listen carefully; learn how to hear God!

He says, "Be still, and know that I am God; I will be exalted among the nations, I will be exalted in the earth." (Psalm 46:10)

"Come to me, all you who are weary and burdened, and I will give you rest." (Matthew 11:28)

Plug into God's power through prayer

Be specific in your prayer requests; pray about everything, asking for God's perfect will.

Do not be anxious about anything, but in every situation, by prayer and petition, with thanksgiving, present your requests to God. And the peace of God, which transcends all understanding, will guard your hearts and your minds in Christ Jesus. (Philippians 4:6–7)

Slow down long enough to hear God's answer

We can become impatient. We want our prayers answered now! We need to remember that our timing can be flawed, while God's timing is perfect!

There is a time for everything, and a season for every activity under the heavens. (Ecclesiastes 3:1)

I wait for the LORD, my whole being waits, and in his word I put my hope. (Psalms 130:5)

Enjoy your growth

Rejoice and celebrate the small successes along your *road to recovery*! Always remember you're on a journey, a journey of several steps. Maintaining an "attitude of gratitude" is like taking spiritual vitamins.

Share your victories—no matter how small—with others in your group. Your growth will give others hope!

Rejoice in the Lord always. I will say it again: Rejoice! (Philippians 4:4)

Rejoice always, pray continually, give thanks in all circumstances; for this is God's will for you in Christ Jesus. (1 Thessalonians 5:16–18)

Here are a few final suggestions for preventing relapse:

1. Pray and read your Bible daily. Establish a specific time of day to have your "quiet time."
2. Make attending your recovery meeting a priority. Stay close to your support team.
3. Spend time with your family (if they are safe). If they are not, spend time with your church family.
4. Get involved in service. Volunteer!

Write About It

1. What does relapse look like for you in your area of recovery?

RELAPSE

2. What are some of the ways (tools) that you have developed in your recovery to prevent relapse?

3. Do a **H-E-A-R-T** check right now. Are you. . .
   Hurting?

   Exhausted?

   Angry?

   Resentful?

   Tense?

4. Specifically, what do you do when you are. . .
   Hurting?

   Exhausted?

   Angry?

   Resentful?

   Tense?

5. Rate your listening skills from 1 to 10, 10 being the best.
   - What are some ways that you think you could improve your listening skills with others?

- What are some ways that you could improve your listening skills with God?

6. Describe what a "quiet time" means to you and why it is important.

7. How could you improve your prayer time? Be specific.

   When do you pray?

   Where do you pray?

8. After you pray, do you slow down long enough to hear God's answer? What does the word "meditation" in this step mean to you?

9. What are some of the other things that you do in your recovery to help you on your journey and prevent relapse?

10. I think we all agree that recovery is a joy, but it also requires hard work. What do you do to celebrate your recovery—even the small victories?

LESSON 22

Gratitude

Principle 7: Reserve a daily time with God for self-examination, Bible reading, and prayer in order to know God and His will for my life and to gain the power to follow His will.

Step 11: We sought through prayer and meditation to improve our conscious contact with God, praying only for knowledge of His will for us and power to carry that out.

Let the message of Christ dwell among you richly. (Colossians 3:16)

Think About It

One of the greatest ways to work Principle 7 and to prevent relapse is to maintain an "attitude of gratitude."

In your prayers this week focus on your gratitude toward GOD, OTHERS He has placed in your life, your RECOVERY, and your CHURCH.

Be thankful to God

Give thanks to the Lord, for he is good; his love endures forever. (Psalm 107:1)

But be sure to fear the Lord and serve him faithfully with all your heart; consider what great things he has done for you. (1 Samuel 12:24)

Shout for joy to the Lord, all the earth. Worship the Lord with gladness; come before him with joyful songs. Know that the Lord is God. It is he who made us, and we are his; we are his people, the sheep of his pasture. (Psalm 100:1–3)

Be thankful for others

Let the peace of Christ rule in your hearts, since as members of one body you were called to peace. And be thankful. Let the message of Christ dwell among you richly as you teach and admonish one another with all wisdom through psalms, hymns, and songs from the Spirit, singing to God with gratitude in your hearts. (Colossians 3:15–16)

Be thankful for your recovery

Therefore, since we are surrounded by such a great cloud of witnesses, let us throw off everything that hinders and the sin that so easily entangles. And let us run with perseverance the race marked out for us, fixing our eyes on Jesus, the pioneer and perfecter of faith. For the joy set before him he endured the cross, scorning its shame, and sat down at the right hand of the throne of God. Consider him who endured such opposition from sinners, so that you will not grow weary and lose heart. (Hebrews 12:1–3)

GRATITUDE

Be thankful for your church

*Enter his gates with thanksgiving and his courts with praise; give thanks to him and praise his name. For the L*ORD *is good and his love endures forever; his faithfulness continues through all generations. (Psalm 100:4–5)*

PRINCIPLE 7B PRAYER

Dear God, help me set aside all the hassles and noise of the world to focus and listen just to You for the next few minutes. Help me get to know You better. Help me to better understand Your plan, Your purpose for my life. Father, help me live within today, seeking Your will and living this day as You would have me.

It is my prayer to have others see me as Yours; not just in my words but, more importantly, in my actions. Thank You for Your love, Your grace, Your perfect forgiveness. Thank you for all those You have placed in my life, for my program, my recovery, and my church family. Your will be done, not mine. In Your Son's name I pray, Amen.

Write About It

1. Why do you think it is important for you to maintain an "attitude of gratitude" in your recovery?

THE JOURNEY BEGINS

2. In what three areas of your recovery are you especially thankful for God's power? Try to think of areas of growth or positive change in you that only God could have accomplished.

3. Name three people God has placed in your recovery who you are grateful for and why.

GRATITUDE

4. What three areas of your recovery ministry, small groups, or other events are you thankful for? Why?

5. List three things that you are thankful for in your church. Be specific.

6. Congratulations! You have just completed your first gratitude list. Review it. How does it make you feel?

7. Let the individuals on your list know what an impact they have had on your recovery, and thank each of them personally!

GRATITUDE

PRINCIPLE 7B VERSES

All Scripture is God-breathed and is useful for teaching, rebuking, correcting and training in righteousness, so that the servant of God may be thoroughly equipped for every good work. (2 Timothy 3:16 17)

That, however, is not the way of life you learned when you heard about Christ and were taught in him in accordance with the truth that is in Jesus. You were taught, with regard to your former way of life, to put off your old self, which is being corrupted by its deceitful desires; to be made new in the attitude of your minds; and to put on the new self, created to be like God in true righteousness and holiness. (Ephesians 4:20–24)

He says, "Be still, and know that I am God; I will be exalted among the nations, I will be exalted in the earth." (Psalm 46:10)

Shout for joy to the LORD, all the earth. Worship the LORD with gladness; come before him with joyful songs. Know that the LORD is God. It is he who made us, and we are his; we are his people, the sheep of his pasture. (Psalm 100:1–3)

Whether you turn to the right or to the left, your ears will hear a voice behind you, saying, "This is the way; walk in it." (Isaiah 30:21)

Blessed is the one who does not walk in step with the wicked or stand in the way that sinners take or sit in the company of mockers, but whose delight is in the law of the LORD, and who meditates on his law day and night. (Psalm 1:1–2)

Therefore, with minds that are alert and fully sober, set your hope on the grace to be brought to you when Jesus Christ is revealed at his coming. As obedient children, do not conform to the evil desires you had when you lived in ignorance. (1 Peter 1:13–14)

Give careful thought to the paths for your feet and be steadfast in all your ways. Do not turn to the right or the left; keep your foot from evil. (Proverbs 4:26–27)

"Watch and pray so that you will not fall into temptation. The spirit is willing, but the flesh is weak." (Mark 14:38)

Be devoted to one another in love. Honor one another above yourselves. Never be lacking in zeal, but keep your spiritual fervor, serving the Lord. Be joyful in hope, patient in affliction, faithful in prayer. (Romans 12:10–12)

Do not lie to each other, since you have taken off your old self with its practices and have put on the new self, which is being renewed in knowledge in the image of its Creator. (Colossians 3:9–10)

If any of you lacks wisdom, you should ask God, who gives generously to all without finding fault, and it will be given to you. But when you ask, you must believe and not doubt, because the one who doubts is like a wave of the sea, blown and tossed by the wind. (James 1:5–6)

LESSON 23

Give

Principle 8: Yield myself to God to be used to bring this Good News to others, both by my example and by my words.

Blessed are those who are persecuted because of righteousness, for theirs is the kingdom of heaven. (Matthew 5:10)

Step 12: Having had a spiritual experience as the result of these steps, we try to carry this message to others and to practice these principles in all our affairs.

Brothers and sisters, if someone is caught in a sin, you who live by the Spirit should restore that person gently. But watch yourselves, or you also may be tempted. (Galatians 6:1)

Think About It

But in your hearts revere Christ as Lord. Always be prepared to give an answer to everyone who asks you to give the reason for the hope that you have. But do this with gentleness and respect. (1 Peter 3:15)

What does it mean to GIVE?

God first

By placing God first in your life, you will realize that everything you have is a gift from Him. You realize that your recovery is not dependent on material things. It is built upon your faith and your desire to follow Jesus Christ's direction.

He who did not spare his own Son, but gave him up for us all—how will he not also, along with him, graciously give us all things? (Romans 8:32)

"No one can serve two masters. Either you will hate the one and love the other, or you will be devoted to the one and despise the other. You cannot serve both God and money." (Matthew 6:24)

I becomes we

The 12 Steps do not begin with the word "I." The first word in Step 1 is "we." The *road to recovery* is not meant to be traveled alone.

"'Love the Lord your God with all your heart and with all your soul and with all your mind.' This is the first and greatest commandment. And the second is like it: 'Love your neighbor as yourself.'" (Matthew 22:37–39)

Two are better than one, because they have a good return for their labor: If either of them falls down, one can help the other up. But pity anyone who falls and has no one to help them up. Also, if two lie down together, they will keep warm. But how can one keep warm alone? Though one may be overpowered, two can defend themselves. A cord of three strands is not quickly broken. (Ecclesiastes 4:9–12)

Victories shared

God never wastes a hurt! Principle 8 gives us the opportunity to share our experience and victories. "This is how it was for me. . . ." "This is what happened to me. . . ." "This is how I gained the strength. . . ." "There's hope for you."

Praise be to the God and Father of our Lord Jesus Christ, the Father of compassion and the God of all comfort, who comforts us in all our troubles, so that we can comfort those in any trouble with the comfort we ourselves receive from God. (2 Corinthians 1:3–4)

Example of your actions

In James 1:22 it says we are to be "doers of the word." But to be of help to another, we are to "carry the message in all our affairs."

Dear children, let us not love with words or speech but with actions and in truth.
(1 John 3:18)

The Lord spreads His message through the eight principles and the Christ-centered 12 Steps. We are the instruments for delivering the Good News. The way we live will confirm to others the sincerity of our commitment to our Lord, to the program, and to them! That's Principle 8.

"No one lights a lamp and hides it in a clay jar or puts it under a bed. Instead, they put it on a stand, so that those who come in can see the light. For there is nothing hidden that will not be disclosed, and nothing concealed that will not be known or brought out into the open. Therefore consider carefully how you listen. Whoever has will be given more; whoever does not have, even what they think they have will be taken from them." (Luke 8:16–18)

Write About It

1. What does 1 Peter 3:15, "But in your hearts revere Christ as Lord. Always be prepared to give an answer to everyone who asks you to give the reason for the hope that you have. But do this with gentleness and respect," mean to you?

2. How has your attempt to put God first in your life changed your understanding of the word "give"?

3. Ecclesiastes 4:9 tells us that "two are better than one." List specific instances in your own recovery that you have seen this verse in action.

4. What are some of your recent victories that you could share with a newcomer?

5. In James 1:22 we are told to be "doers of the word." How can you be a doer of the word. . .
   - among family and friends?

   - in your recovery group?

   - in your church?

   - on the job?

   - in your community?

LESSON 24

Yes

Principle 8: Yield myself to God to be used to bring this Good News to others, both by my example and by my words.

Blessed are those who are persecuted because of righteousness, for theirs is the kingdom of heaven. (Matthew 5:10)

Step 12: Having had a spiritual experience as the result of these steps, we try to carry this message to others and to practice these principles in all our affairs.

Brothers and sisters, if someone is caught in a sin, you who live by the Spirit should restore that person gently. But watch yourselves, or you also may be tempted. (Galatians 6:1)

THE JOURNEY BEGINS

Think About It

When you reach this step you are ready to say YES to service.

Yield myself to God

Principle 8 sums up the Y: Yield myself to God to be used to bring this Good News to others, both by my example and by my words.

Brothers and sisters, if someone is caught in a sin, you who live by the Spirit should restore that person gently. But watch yourselves, or you also may be tempted. Carry each other's burdens, and in this way you will fulfill the law of Christ. (Galatians 6:1–2)

Example is what is important

Your walk needs to match your talk because your lifestyle reflects what you believe. Does your lifestyle show others the patterns of the world—selfishness, pride, and lust—or does it reflect the love, humility, and service of Jesus Christ?

Let us not love with words or speech but with actions and in truth. (1 John 3:18)

Serve others as Jesus Christ did

When you have reached Principle 8, you are ready to pick up the "Lord's towel," the one with which He washed the disciples' feet in the upper room.

Now that I, your Lord and Teacher, have washed your feet, you also should wash one another's feet. I have set you an example that you should do as I have done for you. (John 13:14–15)

How You Can Say YES

1. *Be an accountability partner.* Look for someone in your step study who will agree to encourage and support you as you work through the principles. You agree to do

the same for that person. You hold one another accountable for working an honest program.
2. *Be a sponsor.* Sponsors are people who have worked the principles or the steps. Their job is to guide newcomers on their journey through the program, to give a gentle nudge when they are procrastinating or slow them down when they are rushing through a step. Sponsors do so by sharing their personal journey on their *road to recovery.*
3. *Be involved in Celebrate Recovery and your church.* There are many opportunities for service in this recovery ministry and in your church.

You have come to the fork in your *road to recovery.*

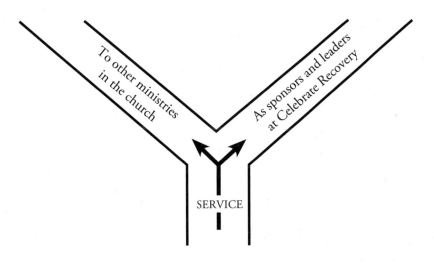

Remember, "You can't keep it unless you give it away!"

THE JOURNEY BEGINS

PRINCIPLE 8 PRAYER

Dear Jesus, as it would please You, bring me someone today whom I can serve. Amen.

Write About It!

1. If you knew that you couldn't fail, what would you like to do most for God in helping others?

2. What are some ways you can pick up the Lord's towel (John 13:14–15) today and start serving others?

3. What does the illustration of the fork in your *road to recovery* say to you?

4. In the words of Step 12, how will you "practice these principles in all [y]our affairs"?

5. Describe what the phrase "You can't keep it unless you give it away" means in your recovery.

6. Create your own action plan for Principle 8.
   I am going to explore opportunities to serve in the following areas:

PRINCIPLE 8 VERSES

Praise be to the God and Father of our Lord Jesus Christ, the Father of compassion and the God of all comfort, who comforts us in all our troubles, so that we can comfort those in any trouble with the comfort we ourselves receive from God. (2 Corinthians 1:3–4)

Only be careful, and watch yourselves closely so that you do not forget the things your eyes have seen or let them fade from your heart as long as you live. Teach them to your children and to their children after them. (Deuteronomy 4:9)

In the same way, faith by itself, if it is not accompanied by action, is dead. (James 2:17)

As a prisoner for the Lord, then, I urge you to live a life worthy of the calling you have received. Be completely humble and gentle; be patient, bearing with one another in love. Make every effort to keep the unity of the Spirit through the bond of peace. (Ephesians 4:1–3)

And we all, who with unveiled faces contemplate the Lord's glory, are being transformed into his image with ever-increasing glory, which comes from the Lord, who is the Spirit. (2 Corinthians 3:18)

And let us consider how we may spur one another on toward love and good deeds, not giving up meeting together, as some are in the habit of doing, but encouraging one another—and all the more as you see the Day approaching. (Hebrews 10:24–25)

Be joyful in hope, patient in affliction, faithful in prayer. Share with the Lord's people who are in need. Practice hospitality. (Romans 12:12–13)

Brothers and sisters, if someone is caught in a sin, you who live by the Spirit should restore that person gently. But watch yourselves, or you also may be tempted. (Galatians 6:1)

Two are better than one, because they have a good return for their labor: If either of them falls down, one can help the other up. But pity anyone who falls and has no one to help them up. Also, if two lie down together, they will keep warm. But how can one keep warm alone? Though one may be overpowered, two can defend themselves. A cord of three strands is not quickly broken. (Ecclesiastes 4:9–12)

LESSON 25

Seven Reasons We Get Stuck

As you complete your journey, you will discover the rewards of sponsoring newcomers. Your role as a sponsor will be to help others along their journey on the *road to recovery* by guiding them through the principles and steps. Your task is not to pick them up and carry them through the steps, but to stand alongside them as they complete their journey.

At times, you may need to slow them down when they are moving through the steps too quickly; or you may need to speed them up when they get stuck along the side of the road. There are seven major areas in which I have seen individuals get "stuck" at some point in their recoveries. It is important that you are familiar with each of them so you help them get "unstuck."

You have not completely worked the previous principle

Perhaps you are trying to move through the principles too quickly. Slow down! Give God time to work! Remember, this program is a process.

Since we live by the Spirit, let us keep in step with the Spirit. (Galatians 5:25)

You have not completely surrendered your life and your will to the Lord

Perhaps you are trusting Jesus with the "big" things, but you still think you can handle the "small" things.

Trust in the LORD with all your heart and lean not on your own understanding; in all your ways submit to him, and he will make your paths straight. (Proverbs 3:5–6)

You have not accepted Jesus' work on the cross for your forgiveness

You may have forgiven others, but you think your sin is too big to be forgiven.

If we confess our sins, he is faithful and just and will forgive us our sins and purify us from all unrighteousness. (1 John 1:9)

For he chose us in him before the creation of the world to be holy and blameless in his sight. In love he predestined us for adoption to sonship through Jesus Christ, in accordance with his pleasure and will—to the praise of his glorious grace, which he has freely given us in the One he loves. In him we have redemption through his blood, the forgiveness of sins, in accordance with the riches of God's grace. (Ephesians 1:4–7)

Have you forgiven yourself?
Remember,

Therefore, there is now no condemnation for those who are in Christ Jesus, because through Christ Jesus the law of the Spirit who gives life has set you free from the law of sin and death. (Romans 8:1–2)

You really have not forgiven others who have harmed you

You must "let go" of the pain of past harm and abuse. Until you are able to release it, forgive it, it will continue to hold you as its prisoner.

Be kind and compassionate to one another, forgiving each other, just as in Christ God forgave you. (Ephesians 4:32)

You are afraid of the risk in making the necessary change

You may be paralyzed by the fear of failure. You may fear intimacy because of the fear of rejection or of being hurt again. You may resist change (growth) because of the fear of the unknown.

So do not fear, for I am with you; do not be dismayed, for I am your God. I will strengthen you and help you; I will uphold you with my righteous right hand. (Isaiah 41:10)

So we say with confidence, "The Lord is my helper; I will not be afraid. What can mere mortals do to me?" (Hebrews 13:6)

You are not willing to "own" your responsibility

You need to take responsibility for your past in a broken relationship, a damaged friendship, with a distant child or parent, and so forth.

Search me, God, and know my heart; test me and know my anxious thoughts. (Psalm 139:23)

You have not developed an effective support team

Do you have a sponsor or an accountability partner? Do you have the phone numbers of others in your step study? Have you volunteered for a commitment to your recovery ministry?

Walk with the wise and become wise, for a companion of fools suffers harm. (Proverbs 13:20)

Carry each other's burdens, and in this way you will fulfill the law of Christ. (Galatians 6:2)

Congratulations!

CONGRATULATIONS, YOU DID IT, YOU HAVE COMPLETED ALL EIGHT PRINCIPLES AND ALL OF THE 12 STEPS!

I do not have to tell you that was not an easy accomplishment! There are many rewards found in this Christ-centered program. It is important that you share your "miracle" with others. You are a living example of God's grace. I pray for your continued growth in Christ, your recovery, and your service to others. Below please find Celebrate Recovery's Daily Action Plan for Serenity.

In His steps,
John Baker

Celebrate Recovery's Daily Action Plan for Serenity

1. Daily, continue to take an inventory. When you are wrong, promptly admit it.
2. Daily, study God's Word and pray asking God to guide you and help you apply His teaching and will in your life.
3. Daily, work and live the eight principles to the best of your ability, always looking for new opportunities to help and serve others—not just at your recovery meetings but in all areas of your life.